MYTHOLOGY AND CULTURE WORLDWIDE

Hindu Mythology

JENNY MACKAY

LUCENT BOOKS
A part of Gale, Cengage Learning

GALE
CENGAGE Learning·

Farmington Hills, Mich • San Francisco • New York • Waterville, Maine
Meriden, Conn • Mason, Ohio • Chicago

LIBRARY OF CONGRESS CATALOGING-IN-PUBLICATION DATA

MacKay, Jennifer, author.
  Hindu mythology / By Jennifer MacKay.
     pages cm. -- (Mythology and Culture Worldwide)
  Includes bibliographical references and index.
  ISBN 978-1-4205-1147-5 (hardback)
  1. Hindu mythology--Juvenile literature. I. Title.
  BL1216.M313 2015
  294.5'13--dc23
                                                        2014021882

Lucent Books
27500 Drake Rd.
Farmington Hills, MI 48331

ISBN-13: 978-1-4205-1147-5
ISBN-10: 1-4205-1147-5

Printed in the United States of America
1 2 3 4 5 6 7 19 18 17 16 15

TABLE OF CONTENTS

Map of the Hindu Civilization

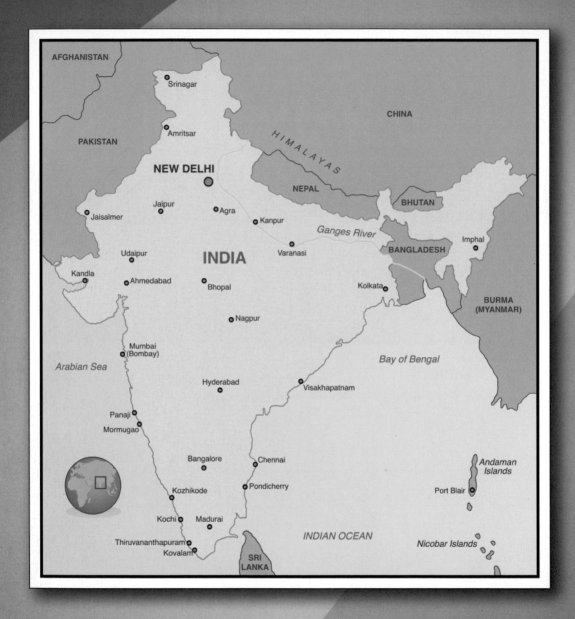

Family Tree of Major Hindu Entities

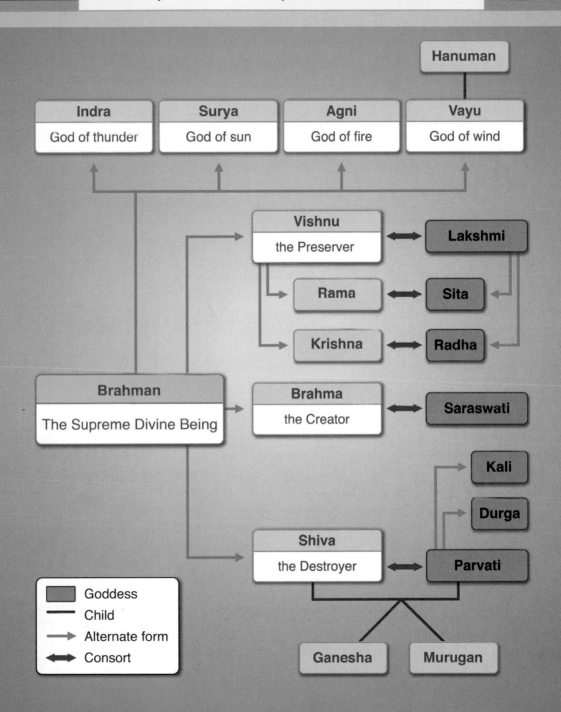

Major Entities in Hindu Mythology

Name of Deity	Pronunciation	Description
Agni	AHG-nee	God of fire and messenger of the gods.
Brahma	BRAH-mah	Creator of the world; one of the Trimurti, the three primary Hindu gods.
Durga	DOOR-gah	Warrior goddess and preserver of righteousness; a form of goddess Parvati.
Ganesha	guh-NAY-sha	Elephant-headed god of wisdom and remover of obstacles.
Hanuman	HAH-noo-mun	Monkey god who helps Rama rescue Sita.
Indra	IN-drah	God of thunder, rain, and war.
Kali	KAH-lee	Goddess of time, death, and war against evil; a form of goddess Durga.
Krishna	KRISH-nuh	Human avatar of the god Vishnu and a hero of *The Mahabharata*.
Lakshmi	LOCK-shmee	Goddess of wealth, prosperity, and good fortune; consort of Vishnu.
Murugan	MOO-roo-gahn	God of war and eternal youth.
Parvati	par-VAH-tee	Mother goddess; consort of Shiva.
Radha	RAHD-hah	Human avatar of the goddess Lakshmi and wife of Krishna.
Rama	RAH-mah	Human avatar of the god Vishnu and hero of *The Ramayana*.
Saraswati	sah-raz-VAH-tee	Goddess of knowledge, music, and creative arts; consort of Brahma.
Shiva	SHEE-vah	Destroyer of the world; one of the Trimurti, the three primary Hindu gods.
Sita	SEE-tah	Human avatar of the goddess Lakshmi and wife of Rama.
Surya	SOOR-yah	God of sun.
Vayu	VAH-yoo	God of wind.
Vishnu	VISH-noo	Protector of the world and preserver of moral order; one of the Trimurti, the three primary Hindu gods.

The Mythical World of Hinduism

In 2009 an Indian elephant shuffled down a crowded street in the New York City neighborhood of Flushing, Queens, to the cheering of thousands of spectators. She was part of a five-day service to consecrate, or make sacred, the recently remodeled Hindu Ganesha Temple that has stood on Bowne Street since 1977. Devoted to a popular Hindu god with the body of a man but the head of an elephant, the temple's elaborately carved walls, shiny golden spires, and statues draped in colorful garlands stand out among the drab gray-and-green buildings of the neighborhood.

The temple is one of thousands of similarly visible centers of Hindu worship in the United States, easily recognized by their elaborate details, bursts of color, and statues of deities. Some of the statues show gods with handsome faces. Others show goddesses, either serene or holding weapons for battle. Some statues have the body of a man but the head of an elephant or monkey. Most have extra arms. Whatever a statue looks like, it is treated as if it were alive. Temple priests adorn it with jewels and flowers and offer it food, and visitors may bow and speak to it. To outsiders, the process and places of Hindu worship can seem foreign and unusual.

To make matters more confusing, different groups of Hindu worshippers gather at different temples, preferring

Members of the Hindu temple in Flushing, New York, hold a celebration to consecrate their remodeled temple. As part of the ceremony, an elephant representing the god Ganesha was paraded through the temple.

to worship one deity over another. To outsiders, it can seem like Hinduism is not one religion at all but many and that its followers worship statues instead of a god. Christians, especially, often find Hindu behavior unsettling, because the Christian holy book, the Bible, specifically instructs them not to worship objects: "You shall not make idols for yourselves, neither a carved image . . . nor shall you set up an engraved stone in your land, to bow down to it."[1] Adding to widespread misunderstanding about Hinduism, the religion has been represented in American cinema as mystical and enigmatic, if not sinister.

The seeming mysteries of Hinduism become much easier to understand once people take the time to explore the culture from which this major world religion comes. Hinduism is rooted in very ancient practices, far older than other widespread religions like Christianity and Islam. At its heart are thrilling myths about the Hindu deities, of which there are many. Elaborate rituals at Hindu temples, popular religious festivals, and even the god statues that Hindus keep in their homes are based on the events of these mythological stories about love and family, good against evil, and living righteously no matter what life brings.

Even Hindus themselves recognize their religion as being very complex. Many believe one requires a wise religious teacher to truly understand Hinduism. The faith is not widely practiced outside India, the country where it originated and where the vast majority of its followers still live. Yet the number of Hindus is steadily increasing, both in India and elsewhere in the world—not because many people are converting to Hinduism, but because the population of existing Hindus is rapidly growing. Already, the influences of this peaceful Eastern religion are more widespread than many people realize. Practices like yoga and meditation, as well as beliefs like karma and past lives, are things Hinduism has shared with the world.

Curiosity about Hinduism has opened many minds to the thrilling and deeply symbolic stories Hindus live by. Fortunately, they are stories Hindus love to tell. Around the world, Hindus and non-Hindus alike can explore and enjoy the exciting realm of Hindu mythology.

CHAPTER 1

Life on the Indian Subcontinent

India, home to the Hindu religion, has had a role in shaping the development of world cultures for thousands of years. Indian civilization existed before the Chinese started building the Great Wall of China around 200 B.C., before the ancient Greeks fought in the Trojan War in the 1200s B.C., and even before the Great Pyramids were built in Egypt around 2550 B.C. While most other ancient cultures have changed or disappeared, the culture of India's native people still exists today and has kept many of its ideas and values through the centuries. "The Indic civilization is incredibly complex," said India culture and history expert Georg Feuerstein before his death in 2012. "India antedates European (or Western) civilization by thousands of years and is in fact the oldest known continuous civilization on Earth."[2]

Written records from many ancient cultures tell how the people of India interacted with the rest of the world and also how other civilizations responded to them. For many centuries India has been a busy trading post and a center of learning. At times it has also been the target of invaders wanting to take it over. India's people often adapted to changes and even accepted the ideas of others without losing their own central values. Many of ancient India's practices and beliefs, including its religion and mythology, are still important elements of Indian culture today. This country of 1.27 billion people, second only to China in population and the largest democratic nation in the world, is a living timeline of human history and especially of Hinduism, the vibrant and colorful religion practiced by 80 percent of all people in India.

The Imprint of Geography

Early Indian beliefs, like those of most ancient cultures, had much to do with the physical features of the land. Covering more than 1.2 million square miles (3.1 million sq. km), India is the world's seventh-largest country in terms of geographic area. It forms a triangle extending off the bottom of Asia into two huge bodies of water, the Bay of Bengal to the east and the Arabian Sea to the west. The Himalayas, the world's tallest mountain range, form India's northeastern border. Pakistan, the country sharing India's northwest border, is the easiest way in and out of India by land. The nation is sometimes called a subcontinent because it is so large and because mountains and water separate it from much of the rest of Asia.

India's unique geography has greatly influenced its people's lifestyle and culture. For example, the Arabian Sea and the Bay of Bengal create unique weather patterns that affect India's climate. For much of the year India is one of the planet's hottest and driest places, but from June to September powerful ocean storms called monsoons blow across the country's southern tip, bringing warm, wet weather and torrents of rain. For thousands of years India's people have relied on this wet season to grow major food crops like rice.

The coming of the yearly monsoons is a reason to celebrate, but monsoons can also be frightening. The fierce storms often bring tremendous winds, crashing waves, and widespread flooding. Indians have long linked the monsoons to the actions of supernatural forces. "The violence and uncertainty of the monsoon create an ever-present psychological factor that may well be related to Hindu ideas about the . . . violence of fate and the gods,"[3] says Hinduism and mythology professor Wendy Doniger. For several millennia, monsoons have helped shape not just cultural practices but religious beliefs in India.

Monsoons affect some of India's people more than others. Much of northern India is in fact a desert, a stark contrast to the tropical coastal areas of the south. In northern India agriculture depends on mountains more than oceans. Melting snow from mountaintops trickles downhill and forms rivers. Two of the most important rivers to the people of India are the Ganges and the Indus, the namesake of India even though most of it is now located in modern-day Pakistan.

As snow melts in the mountains each spring, rivers can carry so much water that they flood when they reach the valleys. When flooding recedes and riverbanks return to their normal levels, they leave behind moist and fertile ground where people grow crops and animals can graze. Like monsoons in the south, the flooding rivers in the north are essential for growing crops. People also use the rivers for travel, and some of India's greatest cities have been built on riverbanks. "Water is so precious in India that rivers are considered sacred," says researcher and writer Bobbie Kalman. "The Ganges is the most holy river of all. According to Hindu legend, the Ganges River once flowed through heav-

Indians have long linked the fierce storms and flooding of the monsoon season to deities and supernatural forces.

en. Many people make pilgrimages to visit holy places along this river."[4] Rivers, like monsoons, are a long-standing source of spiritual beliefs and customs among the people of India.

India also lies in the shadow of the Himalayas, earth's tallest mountain range and another geographic feature that has strongly influenced religious ideas of the country's people. Extending in a 1,500-mile (2,414km) arc along the border between India and its northern neighbors, China and Nepal, the Himalayas' formidable peaks include the ten tallest mountains in the world, including Mount Everest, the world's highest summit. The Himalayas are wide, not just tall. In some places the range is more than 200 miles (322km) across. Only a few passes or roadways traverse the mountains to connect the southern side of the range to the northern, and these can be inaccessible during the winter months when they are buried beneath snow and ice.

The towering, nearly inaccessible peaks of the Himalayas are a source of much mysticism. "Mountains have a particular significance in India," say mythology and geology researchers Edwin Bernbaum and Larry W. Price. "The Himalayas are the home of many Hindu deities."[5] Each year millions of Hindus travel into the mountains on pilgrimages, or religious journeys, especially to the origin of the Ganges River, a site they consider particularly sacred. Many Hindu philosophers, sages, and prophets also travel to or even spend their lives in the mountains. Just as ancient Greeks believed their deities dwelled on Mount Olympus, Hindus regard the Himalayas as the home of many gods. "The Himalayas have lured people to this region since ancient times," says retired economics professor and Hinduism researcher Shantha N. Nair. "For sages, saints and seekers, it is a spiritual [center] beyond comparison."[6]

Mingling with Other Cultures

Throughout history, India's varied climate led to diverse lifestyles for the people who occupied the subcontinent. It became a place of many different tribes or kingdoms, each with its own customs and beliefs. They traded goods, knowledge, and religious ideas with each other and occasionally fought for territory or power, but there was no unified nation of India in ancient times.

A Twisted Symbol

The swastika, the symbol of Nazi Germany in World War II (1939-45), is often associated with hatred and fear, but for thousands of years it has been a Hindu symbol for luck and prosperity. The word *swastika* comes from the ancient language of India and means "it is good."

India's location and climate not only led its native people to live in separate groups, but it also kept the entire subcontinent separate from much of the rest of the world during the early centuries of human civilization. The only ways into and out of India were by sea or the stretch of land to the northwest where the Himalayas do not reach. Historians believe it was by land that other cultural groups first encountered India.

The discovery happened around 350 B.C. The ancient Persians in those days had built a great empire across the modern-day Middle Eastern countries of Turkey, Iran, Afghanistan, and Pakistan. The people of India mingled and traded with these regions to their north. It was only a matter of time until the Greek general Alexander the Great, who conquered all of Persia, led his newly acquired Persian army to the Indian subcontinent. Alexander discovered land toward the south and east—a lot of land. His goal was to rule the entire world, so he immediately invaded India. His seasoned warriors were able to defeat India's small tribes and kingdoms, none of which had an army stronger than Alexander's.

For about two years, from 327 B.C. to 325 B.C., the Greeks fought and conquered various Indian groups. However, India was vast, and Alexander's warriors were tired of fighting. "In July, when the monsoon rains began, the army refused to travel any further in the stifling, humid heat,"[7] says historian Graham Phillips. Alexander gave up on taking over the Indian subcontinent and turned back toward his Greek homeland.

Although Alexander had not succeeded in taking over India, the Greeks did not forget it existed. In fact, historical evidence shows that the people of India and Greece shared ideas and knowledge during their encounters. "Greek culture directly penetrated into western India in the wake of Alexander the Great's invasions," say history professors Paul Vauthier Adams, Erick D. Langer, Lily Hwa, Peter N. Stearns, and Merry Wiesner-Hanks. "Greek artistic themes had powerful influence on Indian art. . . . Greek mathematics and scientific concepts also fed ongoing scholarship with India."[8] These authors note that the Greeks, too, experienced cultural changes from their time spent in India, especially spiritual changes: "Hinduism also won converts, in part because its religion could incorporate different gods and local cult heroes, thus allowing the introduction of some Greek elements."[9]

Centuries later, in 146 B.C., the Romans had taken over the Greek empire and went to India themselves. At that time Roman territory included Egypt on the northeast corner of Africa. From there, sailors found water routes across the Red Sea to the Arabian Sea and on to India. The winds of India's

In 326 B.C. India's King Porus, left, surrenders to the Greek conqueror Alexander the Great.

yearly monsoons brought Roman ships quickly to India's western shores and then pushed them back east weeks later, making trade by sea fast and efficient.

Archaeologists, scientists who study past cultures through the items they left behind, have found Greek and Roman coins buried in India, mixed in with native coins of India and shards of Roman pottery. These artifacts provide evidence that Rome and India mingled often in ancient times. Romans also wrote about the people they met in India, especially the mystics and sages—spiritual leaders who impressed Western visitors with their wisdom. Ancient India, famous for material goods like exotic spices and fancy silk cloth, also became a place of spiritual learning that drew many thinkers and philosophers in ancient times. "For the most part, we think of Hinduism as being confined to India," says Hinduism author and lecturer Linda Johnsen. "However, the further we go back in time, the fuzzier the borders of Hindu culture become."[10]

Muslims Meet the Hindu World

India's exotic landscape, wealth, and wisdom were exciting to the Romans and Greeks, but these same features made India a target for conquering empires. By the twelfth century A.D., the time of the Middle Ages in Europe, the religion of Islam was spreading across the Middle East and into central Asia. Muslims, the name for those who practice Islam, formed great empires. One of these Muslim groups was the Mongols, who fought the Chinese during the twelfth and thirteenth centuries under ruthless warrior kings like Genghis Khan. In the 1500s the Mughal Empire, which had branched off from the earlier Mongol Empire, moved south into the subcontinent of India, where people practiced the very different faith of Hinduism.

At first the Mughals sought wealth and territory and were not interested in other religions. They destroyed many temples and even some cities of India's native Hindu people. But as the years passed, Muslims and Hindus were able to blend their cultures, art, architecture, and religious beliefs into a peaceful and prosperous society. Several Mughal emperors

Manu and the Flood

Hindu myths, like those of many world cultures, include a story of a great flood. India is at the mercy of yearly monsoons—giant tropical storms that bring weeks or months of heavy rain—and experiences many floods. However, Hindu myths tell a story of one particular time when water submerged the entire known world. The only human being to survive was a holy man named Manu, who had once found a small fish in his wash water. The fish begged Manu not to throw him into water with bigger fishes that would eat him, so Manu moved the tiny fish to larger and larger containers of water as it grew. Finally, when the fish was large enough to survive, Manu released it in the ocean.

The grateful fish—who was actually an incarnation cither of Brahma or Vishnu,

according to different sources—returned the favor by warning Manu that a period of heavy rain was coming and would wash away the whole world. Manu built a boat, as the fish had told him to do, and when the floods came he climbed aboard. All other living things were washed away, but the fish, now huge in size, returned and towed Manu's ship to dry land. Once the flood waters receded, the gods gave Manu a wife, and he began to repopulate the earth.

The Hindu flood myth is similar to the biblical tale of Noah and the ark, as well as to other flood stories told throughout the Mediterranean and the Middle East. Some scholars believe that this myth, recurring across so many cultures, suggests there actually may have been a devastating flood in humanity's ancient past, but the matter remains a mystery.

believed in religious tolerance and fairness for all people, and under their rule, Hindus could once again worship freely. For much of the 1500s and 1600s, India was a serene and flourishing place for Muslims and Hindus alike.

These peaceful years came to a halt when a Mughal emperor named Aurangzeb ended the religious tolerance his ancestors had supported. "Aurangzeb ordered Hindu temples to be razed [leveled] . . . images to be destroyed, and Hindu schools to be closed,"[11] says Indian and Hinduism historian Klaus K. Klostermaier. Aurangzeb also heavily taxed anyone in India who was not Muslim. The Hindus grew resentful, and many fought back. It was a time of great social and political unrest. India's people were divided by religious differences, and the nation lacked one strong, central government. Instead, it was separated into many states,

The Mughal emperor Aurangzeb, a Muslim, ended India's religious tolerance when he ordered all Hindu schools closed and Hindu temples and religious images destroyed.

none strong enough to stand up to invaders. The weakened India attracted the attention of nations to the west, organized and powerful countries that had long coveted the exotic resources of the subcontinent.

A European Takeover

By the 1600s Europe was filled with wealthy nations racing to rule the world. Spain, Portugal, France, and England had strong navies and sent fleets of ships across oceans to claim new lands. All four nations knew about the spices, silk, and other exotic wares in India. Weakened by religious struggles among its own people, India was vulnerable to Europeans who wanted it for themselves.

England was the country that finally dominated India. The takeover did not happen the way conquerors of the past had gained control of new lands. Queen Elizabeth I, England's ruler at the time, did not send English soldiers to overthrow the people of India. Instead, the invasion was a business deal. Elizabeth gave money to a massive and wealthy corporation called the East India Trading Company. (A corporation is a company owned by many people or groups that invest money in it.) The company traveled to India and set up bases of operation there in the 1610s.

The East India Trading Company hired its own soldiers, some of whom attacked the people of India and took over entire cities. The company built factories and forced Indians to work in them. By the mid-1700s it controlled most

By the mid-1700s, the British East India Trading Company controlled most of India, taxing the people and punishing those who did not follow its rules.

of India, taxing the native people and punishing those who did not follow its rules. The company also pressured Hindus to convert to Christianity. "Despite the Company's protestations that Indians were free to worship as they wished, Indians began to feel that the Company had broken faith with them," says historian Penelope Carson. "Many Indians came to believe that the British intended to convert them forcibly."[12] From the mid-1700s to the mid-1800s, the British-owned company controlled much of the Indian subcontinent, and its rule created unrest and unhappiness among residents—especially Hindus.

The Fight for Freedom and Democracy

The people of India eventually fought back against the East India Trading Company's harsh tactics. In 1857 they launched a war of rebellion and overthrew the corporation, which was abolished soon afterward. Great Britain promptly took over India's government, however. People from England who had lived and worked in India thought its local customs were barbaric. "British administrators, teachers, and missionaries tended to regard India as a 'backward' country because it lacked Western technology and a highly organized system of government," says English literature and culture professor Jay Stevenson. "They also tended to regard Hinduism in a negative light, failing to appreciate its philosophical principles and condemning many Hindu practices as superstitious and primitive."[13] Believing the country would benefit from exposure to British culture, education, and guidance, Great Britain made India a British colony in 1858. Parliament, the British government, controlled India for the next ninety years.

During British colonization in India, schools were set up to teach children English, modern science, government, and other subjects. However, the British never convinced India's people to give up their most treasured beliefs and customs. In 1919 Indians became desperate for independence from England's laws

Circling Dates

The Hindu calendar is lunar, or based on phases of the moon. A Hindu lunar year is about eleven days shorter than the internationally popular (and sun-based) Gregorian calendar year, so Hindus add an extra month about every three years.

Hindu holy man Mohandas Gandhi led India in a series of nonviolent protests to achieve independence from Great Britain in the early twentieth century.

and rebelled against British rule. Mohandas Gandhi, the most famous leader of the rebellion, encouraged his followers to protest, not through violence but with peaceful methods like boycotts (a refusal to buy goods or spend money on services). The rest of the world came to respect the wise and peaceful nature of Gandhi and of India's people as they calmly fought against British laws.

In time these nonviolent actions led to independence. India became its own nation on August 15, 1947. It went on to establish a republic, a democratic form of government in which people elect leaders to represent them.

A New Era for an Old Culture

Today the Republic of India, as the country is officially known, is the world's most populous democracy and a very diverse place. Technologically advanced cities share the country with monuments, towns, and customs that are many centuries old. Parts of the nation are very modern, but millions of its people still honor traditional customs and beliefs, particularly those of Hinduism, the main religion of India. Today more than 900 million people in India and elsewhere in the world practice the Hindu faith that people of the subcontinent have observed for thousands of years.

Hinduism is always evolving, but many beliefs and practices have been largely untouched by time because Hindu stories have been faithfully and carefully passed down from one generation to the next—at first verbally and eventually in writing. Most major world religions have a sacred book that defines their beliefs—Christians, for example, follow the Bible, Jews the Torah, and Muslims the Koran. Hindus have sacred texts too, but instead of just one book at the center of their belief system, there are many, all used as teaching tools to pass down a way of life. "One of the oldest surviving religions with a literary tradition is Hinduism," say Des Cowley and Clare Williamson, specialists in rare and ancient books. "Its teachings are enshrined within a range of scriptures."[14]

The most ancient written record of early Hindu philosophy is the Rig Veda.

Hinduism has four primary sacred scriptures, called the Vedas. These are the earliest of all the Hindu texts and among the oldest written works in the world. The most ancient is the Rig Veda, a written record of early Hindu thoughts and philosophies. The Sama Veda's religious passages are all meant to be sung and are the original source of most Indian classical music. The Yajur Veda, read mostly by Hindu priests, contains directions for performing religious ceremonies. The fourth Veda, the Atharva Veda, contains passages that are meant to ward off illnesses and disasters.

Each of the Vedas in turn has four main parts. The first is the Samhita, a section of hymns. This is followed by the Brahmana, a section of rituals or chants. The Aranyaka, the third section, holds knowledge meant to be absorbed during meditation. The final section of each Veda, called an Upanishad, helps explain the relationship between people and the spiritual force that guides the world.

The Upanishads are the most widely read parts of the Vedas because they are the easiest for most Hindus to understand. Much of the content in the Vedas is written in hymns (rhyming verses) or chants that are best interpreted by gurus, Hindu spiritual guides whose role is similar to a rabbi among Jews or a priest among Catholics. The Upanishads, though, summarize the main ideas of each Veda and make the Hindu faith more approachable for many worshippers. "We find a major shift in language" between the Upanishads and the rest of the Vedas, says Doniger, "not merely in the grammar and vocabulary, but also in the style, which is far more accessible, conversational, [and] reader friendly."[15] In fact, the word *Upanishad* loosely means "sitting near or beside," as in next to a teacher or guru, indicating that the Vedas are difficult to understand without the help of a religious expert.

The Great Tales of Hinduism

The complex Vedas are the oldest of Hinduism's sacred texts and the ultimate source of Hindu beliefs and practices, but they are not the only texts Hindus revere, or even the most popular ones. Hindus also have texts called Puranas, which historians believe were composed sometime between A.D. 500 and 1500. There are eighteen main Puranas and many lesser ones, but all are collections of Hindu myths about the creation of the world and the lives and adventures of the many Hindu gods and goddesses.

Many Puranas tell stories in the form of conversations between wise men and animals. This format helps Hindus better understand complex ideas and teach beliefs to their children. "Many of these stories have become so popular that they have been staged as dramas [and] cinema and included in our textbooks," says Hindu author and journalist Mahesh Sharma. "They have become . . . part of our folklore by their repeated narration by our 'grandmas' and our 'grandpas' for many a millennium."[16]

Also among Hinduism's most treasured folklore are the two great Hindu epics, long stories told in verse (poetry) about the lives and adventures of major mythical figures. They share similarities with the Greek poet Homer's classic tales, the *Iliad* and the *Odyssey*, but the Hindu epics are even longer. One epic, *The Ramayana*, tells the quest of King Rama, who must reclaim his kingdom and wife when both are taken from him. The other, *The Mahabharata*, tells the story of two families fighting over the same kingdom and of the warrior prince who leads the winning family to victory.

Hindus revere these epic tales and look to them for guidance about making wise choices in life. "They are very popular among the Hindu masses as the repository of great ethical and human values," says philosophy professor Kedar Nath Tiwari. "Presented in the form of stories, both speak of the ultimate defeat of the evil forces by the good."[17] Unlike the *Iliad* and the *Odyssey*, which modern readers consider fictional tales of a culture from the distant past, the Hindu epics are still a central part of Hinduism today.

Out of Many, One

Hindus' sacred texts are full of symbolism and can be read and understood in many different ways. This often makes Hinduism confusing for outsiders. "For all its popularity Hinduism is an elusive religion, and difficult for non-Hindus to understand," says Louise Nicholson, an expert on India's art and culture. Hinduism is also confusing because it seems to be a polytheistic religion, one whose followers believe in

The Sacred Cow

Hindus believe that the supreme divine being can occupy any living thing, so many take care not to harm animals of any kind. Cows are especially protected. Rural families who own cows may treat them as part of the family, and in towns and cities of India, cows often wander the streets without being scolded or chased away.

Many people mistake Hindus' treatment of cows as a sign that they worship these creatures, but Hindus merely believe in showing respect and compassion to animals that generously provide them with many of the things they need to survive: foods like milk, butter, and cheese, and also dung, which is widely used as a source of heat and fuel. For Hindus it is taboo—off limits and offensive—to eat beef or use leather products, but this is not because they think cattle are gods. They simply do not believe in harming gentle creatures who give so much to people.

There is, however, one godly bovine character in Hindu mythology: Nandi, the white bull who is the wise and loyal animal companion of the god Shiva.

Hindus believe in showing respect and compassion to animals that provide them with many of the things they need to survive: foods such as milk, butter, and cheese and dung, which has traditionally been used as a source of fuel for heating and cooking.

numerous gods instead of just one. "Hinduism has no single sacred text, no dogma, no single prophet, and it demands no formal congregational worship," Nicholson says. "Ideas of rebirth and a plethora of deities add to the confusion."[18]

Yet Hindus do not fight with one another over whose favorite god or goddess is the best. Instead, Hinduism is among the world's most accepting religions and accommodates many different beliefs. This is because all Hindus actually do believe in just one supreme, divine being or force that guides the universe. They call this force Brahman, and they believe that all things, living and nonliving, come from and are part of that divine being.

Hindus worship many different gods, but they see these as forms the divine being can take. In essence, to worship one Hindu god or goddess is to worship them all. "Western religions begin with a notion that one—One God, One Book, One Son, One Church, One Nation under God—is better than many," said the late historian Daniel J. Boorstin. "The Hindu, dazzled by the wondrous variety of creation, could not see it that way. For so multiplex a world, the *more* gods, the better!!"[19] As a result of the Hindus' openness to interpreting God in many different ways, Hindu mythology is full of exciting stories about some of the most diverse and colorful characters in the history of human folklore.

CHAPTER 2

Hindu Gods and Goddesses

Most historians consider Hinduism the world's oldest living religion—one that people still believe in and practice. "No world civilization has been as continuous as that of India," says Bansi Pandit, a writer and speaker on Hinduism. "Hindu civilization has not only survived the onslaughts of time, but also is as vibrant today as ever before."[20] On timelines of human history, Hindu beliefs appear earlier than significant events of most other modern religions, such as the birth of Jesus Christ for Christianity or the coming of the Prophet Muhammad for Muslims.

The Hindu concept of time, however, is not a straight line. Hindus envision most things--from the universe to time itself—as part of a cycle. They believe the universe was created long ago and will eventually be destroyed, but these are not one-time events. Much as the earth's seasons come and go, this cycle of destruction and re-creation will continue forever. "The Vedas teach that creation is without beginning or end and appears in eternal cycles of creation and dissolution,"[21] Pandit says.

Life, according to Hindu teachings, follows a similar pattern. Birth and death are not end points on a straight line but part of a recurring process of living, dying, and being reborn. Hindus believe in reincarnation, the idea that after a physical body dies, the soul or spirit that inhabited it can be reborn into another body. These two beliefs—that the universe is repeatedly created and destroyed and that a soul can take many physical forms—help explain how Hindus can believe in Brahman, a single spiritual force or divine being that controls the world, and simultaneously accept the existence of many gods as different forms of Brahman.

In the Hindu worldview, the divine being appears in unlimited ways. "If one were to count all the minor spirits of only local importance as well as the major deities, one could come up with a thousand gods and goddesses at least," says religion professor James B. Robinson. "Hinduism's divine beings are everywhere."[22] These spiritual forms of god have different personalities, talents, and abilities to reflect all the different aspects and capabilities of Brahman.

Hindus also believe that Brahman, the overall divine being, has three primary purposes in the cycle of the universe—to create the world, preserve the peace and prosperity of that world, and destroy the world so the process can start again. These three main roles lead to the Hindu Trimurti, the three major forms Brahman takes in the Hindu belief system: the creator, the preserver, and the destroyer. These are the gods (or the forms of god) at the center of Hindu mythology, and it is from these three that most other Hindu deities take their own forms in the world.

Brahma, the Creator

Brahma is one of the major Hindu classifications of Brahman. The two have similar names, but they are not the same thing. Brahman is the ultimate force present in all things in the world, whereas Brahma is just one form of that force. Brahma is the creator god, the one who made the current world as people know it.

Brahma, like all Hindu gods, is given a human-like image so people can picture him. He is usually shown as a man with four heads and four bearded faces, symbolizing a mature and wise being who watches over all four directions of the world he created. Brahma's heads also stand for the four Vedas, the most sacred texts of the Hindu religion, which were created by Brahma because he knows the origins of everything.

Hindus believe in Brahman, a single spiritual force or divine being that created and controls the world, while simultaneously accepting the existence of many gods, whom they see as different forms of Brahman.

Brahma also has four (or sometimes more) arms, as do most Hindu deities, symbolizing the many special powers he possesses. His hands hold objects that help him in his role as creator, such as a bowl of holy water, a string of prayer beads, and a book or scroll to symbolize the Vedas. In many images he also grasps a spoon to represent the act of pouring oil onto a pyre—a pile of flammable material—to purify a body during Hindu funeral ceremonies, which are meant to send a soul forward to begin a new life. Brahma also may hold a lotus flower, a symbol of purity in Hinduism. Like most of the Hindu gods, Brahma is usually shown with an animal companion—a swan or a white goose that represents knowledge and wisdom.

Brahma is often referred to as the father god. Hindus believe he was the creator not only of the world but of the first human. However, Hindus hardly worship Brahma. One reason is that he has already fulfilled his main role and has little left to do. "Brahma seems to have been thrown into the shade probably because in Hindu mind he has ceased to function actively after creation of the world,"[23] say Hinduism researchers Kailash Nath Seth and B.K. Chaturvedi. Brahma is in a period of rest until the world needs to be created again, so Hindus spend more time worshipping gods who are still active in the world.

Another reason Brahma is less popular than other gods is that he sometimes gives help and favors to characters who later use their new powers to become villains in popular

Brahma is often referred to as the father god. Hindus believe he created the world and the first human.

Hindu stories. "It is more than a coincidence that all the deadly demons . . . received their boons from Brahma which made them singularly notorious in damaging the noble virtues of the world,"[24] say Seth and Chaturvedi. Brahma creates all things in the universe—not just good things but also situations that lead to evil. Such evil is necessary, because without strong villains to fight, mythical Hindu heroes would never accomplish their great victories. Nevertheless, Brahma's often unwitting role in aiding characters who go on to become evil has made him among the least popular of the Hindu gods.

Vishnu, the Preserver

The second member of the three-part Hindu Trimurti is far more significant to most Hindus than Brahma. Once Brahma created the current world, someone had to look after it. That is the role of the god Vishnu, the world's protector and preserver. Among Vishnu's most important responsibilities is to keep a balance between good and evil. He is known for mercy and helps rescue people from the effects of their errors and sins. "Vishnu is one of the most popular Hindu gods today," says Hindu art and symbolism expert T. Richard Blurton. "His devotees believe that at times of spiritual and political decline, he appears on earth as a saviour, guiding erring mankind, benefitting them with an outpouring of his love."[25]

Vishnu is considered an all-powerful and all-knowing deity. He is typically shown with blue skin, since Hindus think of him as being everlasting and existing everywhere, like the sky or the ocean. Images of Vishnu often have three vertical lines painted on the forehead to show that he is one of the Trimurti.

Like Brahma, Vishnu is shown with four or sometimes more arms. In his hands are objects that stand for his most important roles in the world. In one hand Vishnu holds a white lotus flower, symbolizing purity. In another he holds

Once Brahma created the current world, someone had to look after it. That is the role of the god Vishnu (shown), the world's protector and preserver.

a white conch shell, an item that is important to Hindus on many levels but especially because of the humming sound it makes when someone blows through it. Conch shells were used in ancient India to signal the beginnings and ends of battles, and warriors blew through a conch when they were victorious. Hindus also believe the conch makes the sound of the world being created, a sound they know as "om" and often hum during prayers or religious chants. Hindus believe the sound of the conch can ward off evil spirits or save people from disasters. Many of Vishnu's followers believe the conch's sound may even be the breath of the god himself.

Vishnu also carries weapons that he uses to protect the world from evil. In one hand he holds a golden discus, a flat, razor-edged disk that represents the shining power of the mind and also the circular nature of the universe. In another hand he holds a golden club or mace, or sometimes a bow and arrows, all of which represent physical force and power. Vishnu can be a fierce warrior and may use his weapons to fight demons and uphold righteousness.

Vishnu's animal companion is Garuda, a mythical being with the head, wings, and talons of an eagle but the body, arms, and legs of a man. According to Hindu stories, kind-hearted Garuda weighs so much that he snaps the branches off trees. Vishnu's arm, however, is mighty enough to hold him. The two are friends and companions, and images of Vishnu often show him riding Garuda.

Artists also depict Vishnu reclining on the coils of a serpent, often while riding ocean waves. In Hindu mythology serpents often represent the desire for material things like wealth. Such desires distract people from the ultimate goal of Hinduism, which is to disconnect from the material world and find spiritual peace. When Vishnu stands or sits on a serpent, he represents the power to help his followers overcome their dependence on material things, which can be a source of unhappiness in life.

Shiva, the Destroyer

The third major function of Brahman is death and destruction, and this role is embodied by Shiva, the final god of the Trimurti. Shiva's ultimate role is to destroy what Brahma created and what Vishnu protects. To non-Hindus, it may seem as though Shiva would be a fearsome deity and an enemy of Brahma and Vishnu, since his job is to take away life when theirs is to create or protect it. However, Hindus believe that just as the changing seasons bring death to aging plants in the fall so they can bloom colorfully in spring, Shiva's destructive nature allows the whole world to be refreshed.

Hindus revere Shiva rather than dread him. In fact, his name means "fortunate or gracious." He is a necessary and much celebrated part of the Trimurti, for without him, Hindus would have no hope of getting a fresh start. "He is repulsive as well as attractive," says Hindu religion professor Diana L. Eck. "He destroys as well as creates; he wounds and yet he heals. His many weapons . . . make Shiva dangerous and destructive as well as comforting and protective."[26]

Images of Shiva show him in different forms and doing different activities, but he is easy to recognize because of his long, matted hair, often wound into a knot on top of his head. The hair symbolizes the forces of wind that Hindus associate with the breath of life. Shiva wears a crescent moon on his forehead, because the moon's cycles mimic death and rebirth. He is usually shown wearing only a loincloth, the typical dress of an ascetic—someone who has given up the material world in favor of spiritual meditation.

Shiva's body is often covered in ash to represent fire, the method he usually uses to destroy things. He has a third eye in the middle of his forehead, symbolizing that he can see the past, present, and future. This eye remains closed except when Shiva encounters things that displease him. He then opens his extra eye, and flame shoots out to destroy anything in his path. Shiva carries a trident, a weapon with three prongs that stand for the Trimurti, which he can also use to destroy evil with fire. Like Vishnu, he usually has three lines on his forehead to show he is one of the Trimurti.

Shiva usually carries or sits on a tiger skin and has one or more cobras wrapped around his neck to demonstrate his power over fearsome creatures. His animal companion is a white bull named Nandi, who symbolizes snow-covered mountains but also bodily impulses. When Shiva rides Nandi, he shows that he dominates both of those things.

Shiva is a god with a complicated personality. At times he is shown sitting with one leg crossed over the other and his eyes closed, deep in silent meditation and rubbing prayer beads in one of his hands. At other times Shiva dances happily in a ring of flames as he celebrates the destruction of the world. While dancing, he is often shown playing a drum that represents the cyclical rhythm of life and death.

Despite his ruinous reputation, Shiva has a good side. He has been known to help preserve and protect the world if

A River's Fall from Heaven

Rivers have enormous importance to the people of India, and the most sacred of all the subcontinent's rivers is the Ganges. Hindus revere it not just as a river but as a goddess, Ganga. Myths tell how the Ganges, along with India's other rivers, originally existed in the heavens. When the world was created, the soil was parched. Seeing that the world needed flowing water, the gods decided to release Ganga from the heavens. They knew she would cause tremendous flooding if she poured down all at once, however. Their solution was for Shiva to catch Ganga in his long, matted hair and release the water a little at a time. This is why images of Shiva often show him with water flowing from his head.

As with most Hindu myths, this one is meaningful on different levels. Shiva is the god who can destroy the whole world, usually with fire. Ganga, herself a powerful force who perpetually flows from Shiva's hair, helps dampen his fiery personality, just as water soothes and cools. The story is meant to be symbolic more than historically accurate, helping people understand that everything in nature—even destructive forces like water and fire—works to balance other things and can therefore be helpful and protective.

Myths about Ganga have some scientific meaning behind them, as well. She is considered one of the daughters of the god of the Himalayas, which is where the Ganges River originates. She embodies the Hindu understanding that rivers are born in the mountains.

The important River Ganges in India is recognized by Hindus as the goddess Ganga (shown).

it is not time to destroy it. Some images of Shiva show him with a blue stain on his throat, because of a story that he once drank poison out of the ocean to save the world. Shiva usually is shown with one empty hand, which he extends in front of him as a sign that he will protect and bless those who worship him. "He bestows grace," says Eck, "revealing his mercy to his devotees."[27]

This statue represents the preserver (Vishnu), one god of the Trimurti, or triple form, which also includes the creator (Brahma) and destroyer (Shiva).

Hindu Goddesses

Brahma, Vishnu, and Shiva all represent different aspects of Brahman, but Hindus believe the divine being has no gender. "Brahman is neither female nor male but is beyond gender and indeed is beyond description or comprehension by humans,"[28] say religion professors Lynn Foulston and Stuart Abbott. Since males and females are equally important to life and are balanced in the natural world, Hindus believe they must be balanced within Brahman as well. Thus, each of the Trimurti gods relies on feminine power, called Shakti, to blend with and balance his male power. "The energy of *Shakti* manifests itself as a goddess," says Priya Hemenway, an expert on Eastern religions. "It is the complement of the male energy of the triad and is inseparable from it."[29]

To Hindus the Trimurti gods depend on their goddesses, also known as their consorts, just as all life on earth depends equally on females and males. "Without *Shakti*," Hemenway says, "the gods are nonexistent."[30] Each goddess, like each god, is revered by Hindus and represented in a human form with symbols that stand for her special powers or abilities.

Goddess of the Arts

Brahma's consort is the goddess Saraswati. Just as Brahma is believed to have created the first humans, he also created Saraswati from his own body. She is a beautiful goddess, and Hindu legends tell how Brahma was so infatuated with her that he annoyed her by staring at her too much. This is another explanation for why Brahma is usually shown with multiple heads—he is always looking for Saraswati.

As the consort of the god of creation, Saraswati is the goddess of creativity. She represents knowledge, learning, speech, and creative activities like art and music. "All the Indian goddesses are connected to creativity," says spiritual philosophy teacher Sally Kempton. "But Saraswati is the one whose cosmic function it is to embody the creative flow through language, speech, and sound."[31] Hindu artists, poets, musicians, and craftspeople consider Saraswati their muse, and students pray to her for good fortune on tests.

Hindu artists, poets, musicians, and craftspeople consider Saraswati their muse, and students pray to her for help on tests.

Saraswati is elegantly dressed in white. She is often shown sitting on a lotus flower to represent pure thoughts and brilliance. One of her four hands holds a book that stands for learning and knowledge, and another usually holds a string of prayer beads. Her two remaining hands clasp a veena, a stringed musical instrument similar to a lute. The veena is one of the most important musical instruments of India, and Saraswati plays it to show her creative role in the Hindu world.

Goddesses, like gods, have favorite animal companions, and Saraswati's are birds. She is most often shown with a swan to mirror her own grace and beauty. A peacock may also accompany Saraswati, reminding her followers to seek and appreciate beautiful things.

Goddess of Wealth and Prosperity

The goddess Lakshmi, the consort of Vishnu the preserver, represents wealth and protection against misfortune. To Hindus, riches—in the form of money and belongings but also family, friends, and overall happiness—are necessary for life. Lakshmi helps Vishnu sustain the world by providing people with material things they need to prosper and be content. She is one of the best-loved Hindu deities and is especially popular among businesspeople. "Her image is everywhere, associated with wealth, prosperity, good fortune," says women's spirituality expert Karen Tate. "Practitioners who honor . . . Lakshmi with songs, chants, and meditation believe she is generous in her boons."[32]

Lakshmi is usually shown wearing a red gown with gold trim and gold accessories. The gold symbolizes wealth and prosperity, and red is the color of activity—Lakshmi bestows good fortune on people who work hard to earn it. One of her four hands usually pours a shower of coins. Like many gods, she holds lotus flowers in one or more hands and is often shown sitting or standing on a lotus flower to represent that her followers should have pure, unselfish thoughts and not be undone by greed. In fact, Hindus believe Lakshmi withholds blessings, wealth, and prosperity from those who do not work hard or share their good fortune with others. "Though Lakshmi answers prayers, her gifts won't stay with you if you don't practice embodying her qualities—generosity, loving-kindness, balance, carefulness, unselfishness, gratitude, and the more mundane qualities like discipline, cleanliness, and order,"[33] Kempton says.

Lakshmi is usually accompanied by one or more elephants that hold jugs of water or spray water from their trunks. Hindus revere elephants, believing they symbolize good luck and prosperity. Elephants are also associated with

Passionate Pilgrims

The Balaji Temple in the south India city of Tirupati is believed to host more visitors than any Hindu temple in the world. An estimated twenty-five thousand people go to the temple every day. It has six thousand staff members.

rain. Water is sacred in India because without it, food crops cannot grow and people go hungry. The water-spraying elephants that accompany Lakshmi are signs of nourishment and having plenty of the material things people need to survive. Hindus believe that when they worship Lakshmi, she and her elephants will shower them with good fortune.

The Mother Goddess

Of all the Hindu goddesses, Parvati, the consort of the destroyer god Shiva, is thought to be the most powerful. In fact, many Hindus consider Parvati the mother goddess, the source of all other goddesses. Much the way the Trimurti gods are thought to be aspects of the same divine being, Hindus often think of the goddesses Saraswati, Lakshmi, and Parvati as one being: the triple goddess, source of all feminine energy in the universe. Shiva is perfectly balanced by the feminine qualities of Parvati, who helps soften his often fierce impulses. "She is a great force for preservation and reconstruction in the world and as such offsets the violence of Shiva,"[34] says religion professor David R. Kinsley.

According to Hindu myths, Parvati started life as a human. She was born in the Himalayas, and her name comes from the word *parvata*, meaning "mountain." Shiva spends most of his time in the mountains meditating, and one day Parvati saw him and fell in love with him. She was determined to marry him, despite his wild appearance and ways. For a long time he ignored her, but she finally won him over by meditating and praying nonstop to show her devotion.

Parvati encourages Shiva to take part in society and have fun. Shiva's lively dances are one result of their marriage. Hindus sometimes dread his dancing, which can be so energetic that it shakes the earth and oceans, but they believe Parvati helps mellow his emotions and minimize his destructive enthusiasm. A loyal wife, Parvati rarely leaves Shiva's side. Images of her usually show her next to Shiva, often with one of their children on her lap or nearby. She symbolizes female qualities that are important to Hindus, such as being a gentle, loving, and devoted nurturer.

There is much more to Parvati's personality than just doting on her family, however. Hindus believe gods and god-

Religion in Bloom

Many Hindu myths mention the lotus, a type of water lily that grows in Africa, South Asia, and Australia. The lotus has roots in the mud at the bottom of a stream, lake, or pond, but its blooms, which may be pink, blue, or pure white, rest on the water's surface. To Hindus, a lotus blossom represents the soul. A person's body comes from a muddy, soiled world, but the spirit remains pure and clean as it emerges from murkiness and reaches toward heaven.

Images of Hindu gods often show them holding lotuses or sitting on them.

According to myth, Brahma, the creator god, emerged from a lotus plant that grew from the navel of Vishnu, the preserver god. Pictures of Vishnu or his human avatars often show him with skin the color of the blue lotus.

Hinduism is not the only religion to give the lotus a special meaning. This flower has a place of honor in Buddhism, for example, and ancient Egyptians also revered it. For Hindus, as for these other cultures, the lotus is a sacred symbol connecting earth to heaven.

---

desses can take many forms, and Parvati readily branches off into alternate personalities. In one of her forms, Parvati becomes Durga, a mighty warrior goddess who fights the demons of the world.

Demons, like Hindu gods, often take physical forms, but deep down they stand for unwanted qualities like jealousy, greed, selfishness, and prejudice. These are the things Durga combats. "Durga is portrayed as a beautiful golden warrior goddess," say Foulston and Abbott, "but her looks do not belie her excellence in battle."[35] She is usually shown wearing red clothes to signify action and riding a tiger to show her power to subdue fierce opponents. Images of Durga show her with many arms, usually at least ten, to hold different weapons she needs to slay demons. In one hand she often holds a conch shell like the god Vishnu, which she blows to signal victory after a fight.

Durga is a formidable opponent of evil. Sometimes, however, she loses her patience with particularly difficult or troublesome demons. This is when Parvati can take still another form—Kali, a dark-skinned goddess with a terrifying image. Kali is usually shown wearing a string of human

The fierce goddess Kali is usually shown with many arms and wearing a necklace of human skulls and a belt of human arms.

heads around her neck and a belt of human arms at her waist. She holds a bloody knife in one of her many hands and a severed head in another. She sticks out her tongue and often dances on the chest of Shiva, who lies on his back at her feet. "Her unwholesome appearance and strange practices have led many to misunderstand her completely," say Foulston and Abbott. However, they add, "Hindu goddesses cannot simply be taken at face value."[36]

Kali appears dreadful and scary, the total opposite of the loving, motherly Parvati, but Hindus worship rather than fear this form of the goddess. They believe her role is to battle only the most persistent demons—essentially, the most difficult of people's negative qualities. Many Hindus turn to fearsome Kali if they need help with a particularly stubborn personal flaw like jealousy.

Hindus also believe the soul can become a prisoner of the body when someone becomes too attached to his or her physical self. The body parts Kali wears actually symbolize souls she has freed from attachment to their bodies. Outsiders often misunderstand this dark goddess and mistakenly believe that those who worship her celebrate violence and death, but actually, Kali's followers celebrate freedom from negative personality traits. Shiva himself, in drawings of Kali dancing on his chest, looks peaceful because he understands her necessary role in the world.

The Extended Family of Hindu Gods

Hindus worship many more gods and goddesses than the Trimurti and their consorts—thousands or even millions more. Hinduism has deities for countless occasions, natural phenomena, and character traits. There are gods and goddesses of nature and geographic formations as well as of healing, humor, hope, courage, chaos, revenge, gambling, and lost things.

The seemingly endless variety of the Hindu pantheon, or family of gods, leads many who are outside the religion to believe that Hindus are confused about God or do not take the idea of him seriously. On the contrary, Hindus have a very clear idea at the center of all their religious beliefs: There is actually only *one* god, a divine force that is everywhere and in everything all at once. The Hindu deities are all connected, their powers coming from the same source that can do and be anything. The different names, images, and stories of deities are simply the many ways Hindus have invented to better understand the infinite divine being that creates, preserves, destroys, and performs every other function in the universe.

CHAPTER 3

Hindu Heroes and Epic Tales

Hindus worship many different gods, often in different ways, but certain beliefs bring them together as followers of a common faith. Many of these beliefs come from mythological stories countless generations of Hindus have told to their children and grandchildren. "Hindus devotedly and almost unfailingly follow rituals and disciplines handed down to them through oral traditions for thousands of years,"[37] says world religions professor Madasamy Thirumalai. Some myths are told so often and believed so widely among Hindus that they bring even the most diverse and widespread followers together.

The Hindu myths are popular in part because they are very entertaining. Like the fairy tales that are so well known in Europe and the United States, Hindu stories have handsome princes and beautiful princesses, loyal friends, and wicked villains. They take place in glittering kingdoms and sinister forests. Their heroes battle evil and win. There is more to Hinduism's treasured stories than entertainment, however. They represent the way Hindus believe all people should live. To understand Hinduism is to know its ancient myths, starting with the two most important and revered Hindu stories of all—*The Ramayana* and *The Mahabharata*.

The Tale of Rama

Hindus have told of King Rama's adventures since at least 500 B.C., when a Hindu author named Valmiki is said to have written the story down and called it *The Ramayana*. The tale was passed down orally for countless generations so that Hindus who were not literate could still enjoy it. Even today Hindu children know *The Ramayana* before they can read and write, and many can recite parts of it from memory.

Long ago, the story goes, there was a king named Dasartha who had three wives. All three gave birth to sons, and the firstborn of these was named Rama. As Rama grew up, he demonstrated kingly traits. He was honest, fair, brave, and strong. Rama's father wanted him to rule their kingdom of Ayodhya, and so did the people. However, Kaikeyi, one of Dasartha's other wives, thought her own son should be king. Many years before, Dasartha had promised Kaikeyi two favors. She now requested that he grant them. "The first thing I ask is that you make my son, Bharata, the yuvraj (king)," Kaikeyi said. "The second thing I ask is that you banish Rama

An eighteenth-century illustration depicts the marriage between Rama and Sita. Sita would later accompany Rama into exile.

to the forest for fourteen years."[38] According to Hindu custom, a royal person who stayed away from home for fourteen years lost his birthright to claim the throne.

Hindus value keeping their word, so Dasartha had to honor his promise to his wife. Similarly, like all good Hindu sons, Rama had to obey his father's wishes. So he left home. Rama's beautiful wife, Sita, and his other half brother, Lakshmana, insisted on accompanying him into exile.

The evil king Ravana confronts Rama and Sita during their exile. Mesmerized by Sita's beauty, Ravana kidnaps her and takes her to his island kingdom of Lanka.

During Rama's banishment from the kingdom, an evil king named Ravana learned that Rama and Sita were wandering in the forest. Sita's beauty was legendary, and Ravana wanted her for himself. His helpers distracted Rama and Lakshmana, and Ravana kidnapped Sita and took her to his island kingdom of Lanka. Rama and Lakshmana needed an army to rescue Sita, and they found allies in a kingdom populated by the Vanara, a race of people with monkey-like qualities. Among the Vanara, Rama found one of his most faithful friends, a monkey named Hanuman. With Hanuman's help,

Rama declared war on Lanka, killed the evil king, and rescued his wife.

Unfortunately, Rama's troubles were not over. He feared that during Sita's imprisonment on Lanka, she was unfaithful to him. To prove her honesty, he forced her to undergo a trial by fire. If she walked through the flames without being burned, Rama would know that she had remained faithful. Sita passed the test, modeling what Hindus believe to be the perfect virtues of a true and loving wife. Rama realized his suspicions were unfair. "You are my beloved wife and I know your heart belongs to me," he said to Sita. "But I had to do this to show the world how pure you are, and I hope you will understand and forgive me."[39] Together, Sita and Rama returned to the kingdom of Ayodhya, where Rama's half brother Bharata honored him by stepping aside to allow Rama and Sita to take their rightful place as king and queen.

Rama Around the World

Rama and Sita represent values and character traits Hindus believe all people should strive for, such as keeping one's word and honoring marriage vows. "The key characters of this narrative are all shining examples of virtue,"[40] say folklore and mythology experts Philip Wilkinson and Neil Philip. The idea of a prince who is kept from taking his rightful place as king is a popular theme in myths and fables from around the world. The Ramayana is especially important, however, because Hindus believe Rama is not just any prince. He is actually the god Vishnu, and his wife, Sita, is the goddess Lakshmi. Gods, in Hindu tradition, can live on earth as men and women. Their human forms are called avatars or incarnations (spirits that take the form of flesh). Rama and Sita have become part of the folklore of Vishnu and Lakshmi, and their story is sacred to Hindus.

Although The Ramayana is among the most honored stories of Hinduism, it is not always told exactly the same way. Hindus in various parts of India and around the world may

Many Words of Wisdom

*T*he *Mahabharata*, believed to be the longest single work ever written, is seven times the length of the ancient Greek poet Homer's epic poems the *Iliad* and the *Odyssey* combined.

tell different versions. The story also does not feature perfect heroes. Even though Rama and Sita are widely considered to be Vishnu and Lakshmi in the flesh, they have flaws, such as Rama's distrust of Sita. Still, Hindus use the epic story to teach about morals and living the right way. "Not even Aesop's fables or the often intensely moral Greek myths shape the daily lives of present-day inhabitants of Greece," says author and journalist Pankaj Mishra. "In contrast, *The Ramayana* continues to have a profound emotional and psychological resonance for Indians."[41]

A Tale of Two Families

The Ramayana shares its importance among Hindus with another epic story, *The Mahabharata*. Historians believe that *The Mahabharata*, like the tale of Rama and Sita, has been shared orally since ancient times, at least as early as 400 B.C. The first known written version was created around A.D. 400, and *The Mahabharata* became the wordiest story ever recorded. "This epic is unarguably one of the mightiest literary creations in human history, and certainly the longest," says psychology professor Lakshmi Bandlamudi. "Every human dilemma and conflict finds expression in this epic."[42]

The central story of *The Mahabharata* is a feud between two groups of cousins, the Pandavas and the Kauravas. The five Pandavas are the sons of gods. The one hundred Kauravas are born of demons. For many years the families fight over who will rule the kingdom of the grandfather they have in common. Both families become tangled in love triangles, sorcery, curses, and bad omens.

Finally, the Pandavas and the Kauravas meet in an epic battle, an event that some historians believe actually may have occurred in India around 3100 B.C. As the armies prepare for the clash, Arjuna, the best warrior of the Pandavas, balks at the idea of killing his own cousins. He shares his doubts with a friend named Krishna, who has joined the Pandavas to help them fight. "I see omens of chaos, Krishna," Arjuna says. "I see no good in killing my kinsmen in battle."[43] Krishna explains to Arjuna that the battle is not just a human skirmish over a piece of land but a cosmic struggle between right and wrong. Chaos, he says, threatens to take over, and

Arjuna is merely an instrument to help put the world back to the way it was meant to be. "Even without you," Krishna says, "all these warriors arrayed in hostile ranks will cease to exist."[44]

Arjuna realizes that killing his own cousins is a temporary concern, since all people eventually die anyway. The more important issue is battling evil, and it is Arjuna's duty to take action. With Krishna's help, the Pandavas win the battle, retake their kingdom, and restore order to the world.

For Hindus, *The Mahabharata* is much more than a story about a feuding family. In fact, the story of the war between cousins is only about one-fifth of the entire *Mahabharata*. The epic takes many detours to explain various myths and historical characters important to Hinduism and India. Above all, *The Mahabharata* serves as a guide to Hindus about doing their moral duty, a concept known as dharma. "At the very outset the reader is invited to enter the plot and undertake the journey to explore notions of *Dharma*," Bandlamudi says. "In Hindu philosophy, this concept embraces truth, justice, duty, rights, and responsibilities."[45]

A Hindu temple mural depicts Arjuna and Krishna in their war chariot. The two are central figures in the Hindu spiritual epic The Mahabharata.

The most famous and revered part of *The Mahabharata* is the *Bhagavad Gita*, the section of the story when Krishna (whom most Hindus believe is actually an avatar of the god Vishnu) convinces Arjuna to fight his cousins. The discussion is lengthy and explains in great detail the Hindu concept of doing the right thing. The *Bhagavad Gita*, though only one portion of the entire *Mahabharata*, is universally important to Hindus. "Due to its major influence, it is sometimes called 'The Hindu Bible' or even 'The Indian Bible,'" says culture and religion expert Ithamar Theodor. "Moreover, innumerable people worldwide are able to quote it."[46]

Modern Hinduism is largely based on the events of *The Ramayana* and *The Mahabharata*. The epics are full of romance, magic, and adventure, which helps explain their enduring popularity; but to Hindus they are also history books, sources of spiritual guidance, and teachers of right and wrong. Hindus base daily habits and customs on these tales, raise their children according to the values they contain, and plan important festivals around them. *The Ramayana* and *The Mahabharata* are the literary centerpieces of this major world religion.

A Tale with a Tail

The Hindu epics are not just about Rama and Krishna, avatars of Vishnu. They are also the source of mythical tales about other gods with smaller roles in the universe. One such god is Hanuman, the monkey-like being who helps Rama rescue Sita. Hindus consider Hanuman a lesser god than the Trimurti, but that has done nothing to diminish his overwhelming popularity. Many Hindus worship and revere Hanuman as much as—and sometimes even more than—Rama himself, to whom Hanuman swears eternal devotion. "Hanuman's devotees often point out, with a touch of both irony and satisfaction, that there are, in most regions of India, far more shrines to Hanuman than to his exalted master,"[47] says Hinduism professor Philip Lutgendorf.

Laser Focus

Scientists at the Lawrence Livermore National Laboratory in California developed a powerful, twenty-beam laser in 1977. They named it the Shiva Laser after the Hindu destroyer god Shiva, who can open his third eye and annihilate anything in sight with a beam of fire.

A statue memorializes Hanuman, the monkey god who helped Rama rescue Sita in the Hindu epic The Ramayana.

Hanuman, according to *The Ramayana*, is the son of a Vanara (monkey) mother, but his father is Vayu, the god of wind. Like all beings who are half god and half earthly creature, Hanuman is born with special powers. His monkey-like traits make him a playful and sometimes mischievous child, but he also has superhuman strength. One day he decides to leap up and remove the sun from the sky to play with it. This alarms Indra, the god of thunder, who strikes Hanuman down with a lightning bolt. Hanuman survives the incident but bears a lifelong scar on his chin, which can be seen in

The Power of Seven

Hindus believe each person's soul is on a journey of learning to live righteously and detach from worldly things. It may take many lives to learn how to separate the soul from the body, but those who eventually master the skill can help teach it to others. These people become gurus, or spiritual teachers, and Hindus seek them out so they, too, can earn *moksha*—the liberation allowing one to merge with the divine being after death instead of being repeatedly reborn into a new physical body.

Some Hindu gurus are believed to have been so successful at mastering their spiritual selves that they are revered almost as much as gods. These highly accomplished gurus are called rishis. Hindus believe rishis have the freedom to move at will between the spiritual world of the gods and the physical, human world but prefer to live among people and help others achieve spiritual freedom.

Rishis are characters in many Hindu myths. One of the most popular comes from *The Mahabharata* and tells of seven ancient rishis who became the seven stars of the Big Dipper. Hindu mythology calls the constellation the Saptarishi (literally, the "seven rishis"). Able to move freely between earth and the heavens, these seven rishis brought knowledge and the promise of spiritual bliss to mankind. They have a parallel in ancient Greek mythology, which also mentions seven wise men who were the founders of Greek mythology.

most drawings or images of him. The severe punishment also earns Hanuman the pity of the gods, who give him other special powers. He is able to shrink or grow to any size, go anywhere in the world, and even create and destroy things.

These gifts do not make Hanuman evil or greedy, as sometimes happens in Hindu mythology to those who are granted special powers from gods. Instead, Hanuman develops values that Hindus greatly admire. He is intelligent, well spoken, patient, and modest. When Rama meets Hanuman for the first time in *The Ramayana*, he is impressed by the monkey's character. Hanuman, likewise, recognizes Rama's godlike qualities and becomes instantly and permanently devoted to him.

Without the help of his faithful friend Hanuman, Rama would be unable to rescue Sita. Only Hanuman knows where the demon Ravana is keeping her. With his ability to go anywhere, Hanuman sneaks into Ravana's kingdom of Lanka and warns the demon king to free Sita or face Rama's wrath. Ravana's men capture Hanuman and set him on fire, but using his ability to shrink and grow at will, Hanuman scampers around Lanka with his tail ablaze, setting fire to the whole city before escaping and returning to Rama. Later, during the battle between Rama's and Ravana's armies, Rama's half brother Lakshmana is badly injured. Hanuman demonstrates his heroic qualities once more, making a difficult and dangerous journey to bring back the only medicine that can save Lakshmana's life.

Without Hanuman, *The Ramayana* would not have a happy ending. The monkey-god is therefore one of Hinduism's most beloved characters. Hanuman demonstrates many qualities and values that are important to Hindus, such as being wise and fearless, but his most important trait is his devotion to Rama and Sita. Many images of Hanuman, who is easily recognizable because of his monkey-like face and tail, show him pulling apart his chest to reveal that Rama and Sita are painted on his heart.

Hanuman, a secondary hero of *The Ramayana*, is one of the best known and widely worshipped of all the Hindu deities. "I have found that Hanuman is, among other things, a deity at the mention of whom people's eyes light up and their faces break into smiles,"[48] Lutgendorf says.

A God from Another Story

The Ramayana and *The Mahabharata* contain many myths about divine beings, but they are not the source of all stories about popular Hindu gods. Another favorite Hindu deity, Ganesha, is not mentioned in the epics but instead comes directly from the Vedas, the most ancient of the sacred Hindu scriptures. Ganesha, however, has much in common with Hanuman, both in features and popularity. As a son of the destroyer god Shiva and his wife, Parvati, Ganesha, too, has the blood of gods, which gives him special powers.

Also like Hanuman, Ganesha appears as a blend of animal and human. Whereas Hanuman has a monkey's face and tail, Ganesha has the body of a man but the head of an elephant. This strange arrangement happened when Ganesha was young. Shiva, Parvati's husband, had no interest in children or fatherhood, so Parvati made Ganesha by herself while Shiva was away. One day she asked her son to make sure no one interrupted her while she was bathing. That same day Shiva, upon returning home from his trip, came across Ganesha, who stubbornly blocked the god's way into his own home. Irritated by the child's behavior, Shiva cut off Ganesha's head.

Parvati flew into a fit of despair. Shiva, realizing he had killed his own child, did the only thing he could to console Parvati—he sent messengers to collect the head of the nearest living thing they could find so he could use it to mend the damage. The head happened to be that of a dying elephant. The revived Ganesha wore the elephant's head from that day on.

To help make up for his mistake, Shiva also blessed Ganesha with special gifts of wisdom and strength, which are fitting for a god with the head of an elephant. Hindus have great admiration for elephants, highly intelligent animals that are strong enough to knock down barriers or defeat any foe but that are also patient, kind, and loving to those who show them affection. Ganesha, in keeping with these qualities, is the Hindu god of wisdom and the remover of obstacles. He is among the kindest and most affectionate of all the Hindu deities. Hindus believe Ganesha's large ears can hear every prayer and request, no matter how small or humble, and that his pot belly is a sign of his power to swallow all the sorrows of the world and help his followers be prosperous and happy.

Ganesha's animal companion is a tiny mouse, which often puzzles people who are unfamiliar with Hindu mythology. The mouse symbolizes the ego, a person's sense of self-importance, while the much larger Ganesha stands for wisdom. By choosing such a small and unimpressive creature as his companion, Ganesha shows he is humble but also that wisdom can master the ego. Because elephants are known to be startled or unnerved by fast-moving mice, Ganesha's choice of companion may also demonstrate that he does not hide from fears and troubles but instead finds a way to work with them.

Because of his reputation for knowledge and understanding, Ganesha has ties to *The Mahabharata*. Hindus believe the epic was composed by a sage named Vyasa, who asked Ganesha to write down the words as he dictated them. One

A painting of the goddess Parvati and god Shiva with their son Ganesha. Parvati made Ganesha by herself while Shiva was away.

legend says Ganesha believed the task was so important that no ordinary writing utensil would do, so he snapped off one of his tusks and used it to write down *The Mahabharata*. Images of Ganesha usually show him with only one tusk.

Although he is not as powerful as some gods and goddesses, Ganesha is a very popular and important deity. Because he is a keeper of wisdom, many Hindus bless his name before praying or reading from sacred texts. Many also pray to Ganesha, the remover of obstacles, before endeavors such as traveling or starting a new job. Ganesha's likeness frequently appears at or near the entrance to businesses and temples, and his is usually the first image Hindus display in a new home. "Whatever other deities a Hindu may worship," says religious studies professor Paul B. Courtright, "[Ganesha] is worshipped first. He stands at the doorway and allows the devotee access to other deities and whatever blessings may

The Thirst of Ganesha

Just before dawn on September 21, 1995, a visitor to a Hindu temple in New Delhi, India, offered a spoonful of milk to a statue of Ganesha, the popular elephant-headed deity. To the worshipper's delight, the milk vanished from the spoon. Offerings of milk to other Ganesha statues met with the same results. Word of Ganesha's apparent thirst flew across India. Millions of Hindus flooded to temples to see the miracle for themselves, causing traffic jams and milk shortages in metropolitan areas. The seeming miracle was not limited to Asia, either. Ganesha statues as far away as the United Kingdom and Canada sipped milk from spoons and shallow dishes held up to a tusk or a trunk.

Skeptics said the vanishing milk was the result of capillary action: liquid soaks into porous materials that have tiny holes, such as cement or wood, because water molecules tend to stick to each other and to other materials. However, witnesses claimed they had seen milk vanish in front of ceramic and metal statues, which are nonporous. The milk—sometimes gallons of it—also disappeared into statues without a trace, seeming neither to soak the statue nor to dribble out from anywhere. Furthermore, the very statues that absorbed milk that day have never done so again. The worldwide Miracle of the Milk remains an unexplained occurrence. Many Hindus cite it as evidence of their deities' living presence in the material world.

Modern Hindu worshippers in London offer milk before a statue of Ganesha.

flow from them."[49] The elephant-headed god is loved and worshipped by Hindus all over the world. "[Ganesha] is often said to be the most popular deity in the Hindu pantheon,"[50] Courtright says.

Cosmic Myths

Part of Ganesha's and Hanuman's widespread popularity is due to their resemblance of animals. Nature is extremely important to Hindus, and they worship and respect all aspects of the natural world. Many well-known Hindu myths predate even the ancient epics and tell the world how heroes like Rama and Krishna came to exist in the first place. These nature myths have many things in common with the beliefs of other ancient cultures like the Egyptian, Greek, and Roman. Early Hinduism, like many other old religions, sought to explain the natural phenomena of the world by naming gods for them.

Rain was among the first phenomena to which Hindus assigned a god, and they called him Indra. Like the Greek god Zeus, Indra controlled thunder and wielded a lightning bolt as a weapon. Hindus also believed in Surya, the sun god, who was said to ride across the sky each day in a flaming chariot, like the Greek god Apollo and the Egyptian god Ra. Vayu was the often ill-tempered god of wind and air, and Agni was the god of fire. These and other gods were the source of many myths depicting the creation of the world. One Hindu tale tells how gods and demons, in a battle for power over the universe, began to churn the ocean, spinning it around a central point or pole. Many things emerged from the spinning waters, including certain gods and goddesses as well as landforms, poisons, and precious gems. The churning of the oceans is one way Hindus explain the creation of the world as people know it today.

All stories of Hinduism are rich in meaning and symbolism, and scholars believe ancient Hindus may have had a much better understanding of the natural world than the mythical stories seem to suggest. For example, the churning ocean could mean the literal oceans of the earth, which are actually one continuous body of water that circulates, or churns, around the globe—a fact that humans did not know until thousands of years after the ancient Hindus first told of churning oceans. The churning myth may also have to do with astronomy, since the Hindus also referred to the *heavenly* ocean. "The churning of the heavenly ocean stands for something called 'libration,' the movement of the north celestial pole back and forth across the sky as the Earth wobbles on its axis over tens of thousands of years,"[51] says Johnsen. Early Hindus had many such myths to explain the existence of things in their world, from the night sky to weather to human nature, and many of their ancient stories are consistent with what modern science now knows about the world.

Blending the Old with the New

Hinduism was not the only religion to develop myths in an attempt to explain the world and the place of humans in it, but Hindus today still retell their favorites, whereas the stories of other cultures like the ancient Egyptian and Greek have fallen into history. Even though Hindus still share imaginative stories about gods, however, their culture is not as superstitious and primitive as outsiders sometimes believe. India is home to cutting-edge cities with universities, hospitals, and research facilities. India's citizens, most of whom are Hindu, are known for keen intelligence, inventiveness, and creativity. Hindus have great respect for the natural world, and most Hindus believe modern knowledge can exist peacefully alongside the stories their ancestors have told for thousands of years.

"The ancient world did not artificially divorce spiritual wisdom from scientific knowledge," said India culture and history expert Georg Feuerstein. "There were no watertight compartments of knowledge but various areas of understanding with permeable boundaries."[52] Hinduism today still allows believers to blend traditional beliefs with new discoveries about science and the world. For Hindus, celebrating deities in traditional ways does not conflict with taking part in contemporary life.

CHAPTER 4

Worshipping the Pantheon of Hindu Gods

Hinduism fits as well in the modern world as it did in the ancient one, in part because it does not dictate many specific practices or behaviors that all worshippers must follow. Instead, Hindus are welcome to believe in different gods, read different sacred texts, and worship in different places and different ways (or in no particular way at all). This flexibility may be one reason why Hinduism has stood the test of time, but it also makes Hinduism so complex that it often baffles followers of other religions who try to understand it.

"Even to talk of a single something called Hinduism can be misleading," says religion professor Ninian Smart, "because of the great variety of customs, forms of worship, gods, myths, philosophies, types of ritual, movements, and styles of art and music contained loosely within the bounds of the religion."[53] Hindus believe there is one all-powerful spiritual force, Brahman, but it can manifest, or display itself, in nearly as many ways as a human mind can invent. To Hindus there might be as many different gods as there are people—and as many different ways to worship them.

As long as a person worships with an open and honest heart, Hindus believe, Brahman will hear and understand the prayer. Most Hindus do, however, find that a certain god, goddess, or belief makes more sense or has more appeal to them than others. Certain Hindu deities are more popular than others, too, and Hindus tend to form groups based on the deities they believe are the best or most important. Most Hindus belong to one of the four major branches, or denominations, of Hinduism: Vaishnavism, Shaivism, Shaktism, and Smartism. Each of these has unique beliefs, practices, holy sites, and festivals, but they all exist together peacefully in a religion that allows people to express their faith in numerous ways. "All these denominations subscribe to the broad basic beliefs and

An illustration of several Hindu deities.

principles of Hinduism," says Hindu priest Amrutur V. Srinivasanp. "Hinduism proclaimed early its openness in allowing and welcoming different approaches to salvation."[54]

Devotees of Vishnu

The most popular denomination of Hinduism is Vaishnavism. Its followers, called Vaishnavas, believe that Vishnu is the most powerful and important deity. Although Vaishnavas may also admire and worship other deities, they believe the other gods are different forms of Vishnu, come from Vishnu, or that the spirit of Vishnu has entered them. According to followers of this denomination, the all-knowing and all-powerful force many Hindus call Brahman is actually Vishnu, the preserver god.

Vishnu's consort, the goddess Lakshmi, is important to Vaishnavas, too. "In all his incarnations, *Lakshmi* accompanies *Vishnu*," says Hinduism expert Vensus A. George. "She is ever at his side in every form *Vishnu* takes."[55] Because gods are considered inseparable from their consorts, like two halves of the same being, many Vaishnavas worship Lakshmi equally as a part of Vishnu himself.

Vaishnavas believe Vishnu has appeared on earth at least ten times to help correct chaos during periods when he sees evidence that evil forces threaten to overpower spiritual people trying to do the right thing. According to ancient Hindu texts, the most recent appearance of Vishnu in human form was about the sixth century B.C. Hindus believe he will eventually come to earth in human form once more when the world's people have forgotten completely about spirituality and responsibilities. His return will mark the ending of the current era of human history.

The two best-known avatars of Vishnu are Rama, the hero of *The Rumayana*, and Krishna, the warrior and adviser who shares his wisdom in *The Mahabharata*. Within Vaishnavism there are further divisions, or sects. Some of these worship Vishnu primarily in the form of Rama (along with his wife, Sita, an avatar of Lakshmi). Others worship Krishna (paired with his wife, Radha, another avatar of Lakshmi) as Vishnu's most divine form. Some Vaishnavas worship one of Vishnu's

The denomination of followers of Vishnu, called Vaishnavas, is the largest branch of Hinduism. Here, Vaishnavas worship at a temple in India.

other avatars, and some prefer to think of Vishnu in his god form rather than as a human avatar.

Although Vaishnavas may disagree about which form of Vishnu is supreme, certain religious practices identify them all as devotees of Vishnu over other deities. They often draw marks on their foreheads, for example, to show their reverence for Vishnu and Lakshmi. White lines in the shape of a *U* or a *V*, sometimes with a red dot in the middle, symbolize the feet of Vishnu. These forehead marks are popular symbols among Vaishnavas, many of whom like to publicly show their devotion to their chosen god.

Vaishnavas believe Vishnu and Lakshmi truly care for them and that faithful followers become the god and goddess's human companions. This makes Vaishnavas very loyal to their chosen deities. They read the stories of Vishnu's avatars and feel a connection to or even a friendship with him. "Love is the vital force of [Vaishnavism]," says Ajit Mookerjee, who specializes in the sacred texts of India. "Fervent devotion to a personal god . . . is one of the paths to liberation."[56]

Followers of Shiva

The second-most popular denomination of Hinduism is Shaivism. Its followers, Shaivas, are people who worship Shiva above all other gods. Although many more Hindus are Vaishnavas than Shaivas, historians believe Shiva's denomination is the oldest branch of Hinduism. Shiva and his consort, Parvati, are at the center of Shaiva beliefs and practices.

Shiva's ultimate role, his followers believe, is to free them from their attachment to their earthly bodies. Asian religions professor Ginette Ishimatsu explains the belief in Shiva this way:

> Shiva is the ultimate god who is omniscient, omnipotent, and eternally liberated. Souls, too, have most of the same inherent qualities, but, caught in a state of spiritual bondage, they do not realize their true nature. Out of his grace, Shiva creates the universe through the agency of divine beings in order to provide the conditions for souls to find release from the shackles of ignorance.[57]

Sometimes it takes fierceness to combat unwanted traits like ignorance, and those who worship Shiva and Parvati look upon their favored deities as allies to help them battle their own personal demons.

Shaivas do not believe that people are Shiva's companions. Instead, they believe Shiva is a part of them, and their ultimate goal is to make a spiritual connection with his presence. Shaivas therefore tend to study the holy scripture of the Vedas more than other Hindu texts. They spend more time on meditation than Vaishnavas do, and they take spiritual pilgrimages—especially to the site in the Himalayas where Shiva and Parvati are said to make their home. Shaivas also make pilgrimages to one of Hinduism's holiest places, the city of Varanasi on the banks of the Ganges River in northern India. Varanasi, also sometimes called Benares, is known as India's religious capital. According to

Forehead Decor

Bindi is the name for the dot many Hindu women make between their eyebrows. Often used as a beauty mark, it can also represent the intellect or symbolize a third eye (like Shiva's) to be used for looking inward and meditating.

Hindu legend, its location on the Ganges is where Shiva and Parvati stood at the very beginning of time as the world was created. Visitors to this ancient city come for many reasons, but Shaivas especially travel there to connect with their chosen deity.

In addition to showing their devotion by making pilgrimages, some Shaivas draw horizontal lines of ashes on their forehead to symbolize Shiva, who himself is usually shown covered in ashes. "The ashes smeared on the body remind one that death is the ultimate reality of life," says Hinduism teacher Prem P. Bhalla. "One comes from the earth and returns to it after death."[58] Ash, to Shaivas, symbolizes Shiva's main role in life and the universe.

Shaivism is an intellectual and abstract branch of Hinduism, and Shaivas tend to worship god as a symbol or an idea rather than a man. This is one main difference between them and Vaishnavas, who often worship Vishnu in his human forms. Shaivas do, however, revere certain images of Shiva and Parvati, especially those that show the couple as loving parents. The elephant-headed Ganesha, one of the sons of Shiva and Parvati, is especially popular among Shaivas.

Goddess Worshippers

The third major denomination of Hinduism is Shaktism, consisting of people who worship the female aspect of Brahman, known as Shakti or Devi. There are many Hindu goddesses, but Shaktas considered Shakti as the source of all of them. From another viewpoint, all goddesses are different personalities of Shakti. Shaktas worship what they refer to as the Mother Goddess or the Divine Mother. The entire universe, they believe, came from feminine energy, much the way all living creatures are born from females. "In the broadest sense, Shaktism refers to the worship of *shakti*, the primordial feminine power that creates, maintains, and reabsorbs the universe in the form of a personal supreme Goddess, who is understood to encompass all,"[59] says religious studies professor Carlos Lopez.

Hinduism's fiercest deities are females, especially the warrior goddesses Durga and Kali, and Shaktas especially revere these powerful and sometimes frightening forms of

the goddess. They also associate Shakti with both health and disease. They believe epidemics, or widespread illnesses, happen when the goddess is displeased. "We do see the hidden faith of many South Indian villages in considering contagious diseases as the work of certain deities," says world literature professor Stefano Mercanti. "These female goddesses . . . are usually feared for their tremendous energy (*shakti*); . . . [they] are known to be easily inclined to anger and thus need to be constantly pacified so as to avoid incurring their displeasure and making the disease more virulent."[60]

Shaktas worship the mother goddess, or Divine Mother, under her many forms, including the dark Kali (shown).

However, Shaktas also worship goddesses for their gentler feminine qualities such as creativity, patience, generosity, and maternal love. Many Shaktas draw a red vertical line on their forehead to symbolize the singular and loving nature of feminine power. They often visualize Shakti as a coiled serpent within every human being. This serpent must be awakened by meditation and other practices before a person can become enlightened. This is the ultimate goal of Shaktism.

Believers in All

Vishnu, Shiva, and the feminine aspect of Brahman have attracted millions of loyal followers, but Hinduism has many more than three forms of God. The fourth major Hindu denomination, Smartism, encourages followers to worship whatever deity or deities they feel most connected to. The basic idea of Smartism is that all deities are equal, so it makes no difference which one a person chooses to worship.

Smartism is the newest and least traditional of the Hindu denominations. Its name comes from the word *smriti*, which describes Hindu texts that were human-made (as opposed to *shruti*, the Hindu texts that were heard directly from God).

Shruti texts are considered primary sources of Hindu beliefs and therefore can never be changed, whereas *smriti* texts can be added to over time. Smartism follows the *smriti* traditions, making it the most liberal Hindu denomination.

Most Smartas, as followers of Smartism are called, worship one or more of its six primary deities: Vishnu, Shiva, Hanuman, Ganesha, Surya, and Murugan (Ganesha's brother), who is the second son of Shiva and Parvati and represents war and eternal youth. Smartas who follow Vishnu or Shiva are different than Vaishnavas or Shaivas because they believe all gods have equal value and merit, whereas the other denominations think Vishnu or Shiva is the most important god.

Smarta temples feature images or statues of all six of Smartism's main deities and invite visitors to worship any or all of them. In addition, a Smarta may identify with and worship any other deity not among the main six. Although fewer Hindus claim to be Smartas than any of the other main denominations, Smartism reflects the overall belief of most Hindus that the Supreme Being can take any form.

The Height of Hanuman

In 2003 Hindu followers of Hanuman in southeastern India erected a statue of their beloved monkey-faced god that is 135 feet (41m) tall, the height of a twelve-story building. It is the largest *murti*, or statue, in India.

A Faith of Freedom

Although most Hindus feel very loyal to their chosen deity or deities, the denominations accept one another's differences. Hindus are also free to belong to no denomination but instead choose their own gods and methods of worship. Disagreements about religious beliefs are rare among Hindus. This is one major way Hindu worship differs from many other religions—Hindus are very accepting of all spiritual beliefs. According to the editors of *Hinduism Today Magazine*:

> Hindus do not proselytize, meaning they do not try to convert members of other religions to Hinduism. Proselytizing is based upon the belief that one's religion is the only true religion and therefore everyone in another religion should join it. Hindus hold the opposite point

of view, which is that all faiths are good and the members of those religions are just fine remaining in the religions they are in.[61]

Hindus are tolerant and accepting of various views, making India one of the world's most spiritually diverse and active countries.

Statues Everywhere

Hindus worship a wide variety of gods and goddesses, and different towns or regions usually have favorite deities. This is obvious to visitors because images of gods are everywhere—in public buildings, businesses, restaurants, parks, hospitals, and anywhere else a person might go. These images, called

A Matter of Class

For thousands of years Indian—and by extension, Hindu—society has grouped people by birth into social classes, or castes. The most respected caste consists of the Brahmins, who are intellectual and spiritual leaders such as teachers and priests. Next are the Kshatriyas, which include politicians, police officers, and soldiers. Vaisyas are the caste of craftspeople, farmers, and merchants. The lowest caste, Shudras, are laborers, usually unskilled and with little education. Many Indians do not believe in marrying outside of one's caste, and children are expected to remain in the caste into which they were born. There are few opportunities in this system to rise to a higher caste, such as through hard work or education, and this leads many people to criticize the system.

Hindus, however, view the caste system in terms of karma and reincarnation. People who live virtuously build up good karma and believe they will be rewarded by being reborn into a higher caste. People who have bad deeds or thoughts, on the other hand, build up bad karma that may result in spending future lives in a lower caste. Hindus believe that all actions have consequences. Their place in the current life is a result of their behavior in a past one. Sacred Hindu stories like those of *The Mahabharata* teach that whatever people's caste may be, the gods want them to do their dharma, or duty, without complaint. Hindus, therefore, generally accept the caste system because they believe they can rise to a higher level in the next life if they do their dharma in this one.

murtis, are sacred symbols of the deities they represent, and Hindus often worship them by praying to them or leaving them food and other offerings.

Hindus believe the supreme spiritual being is everywhere and in all things at once, so a statue or painting of any god can be a part of the supreme god. Nevertheless, not every image of a god is considered a murti. Every murti must be prepared in a specific way to fully channel God's energy. Statues are usually made of stone, metal, wood, or clay, and if the murti is a painting, it requires certain colors. Murtis, whether paintings or sculptures, must have a specific shape and precise dimensions. Different deities are shown in particular postures, and the position of a murti's hands is very important. Sacred Hindu texts contain directions for making murtis, and it is an honored craft.

A sculptor or artist does not work alone in the making of a murti. A sage, or spiritual guide, performs special chants at different points in the process and must invoke, or summon, the presence of God into the image once it is complete. "From this moment, what was merely dead wood or stone becomes for the worshiper a sacred icon and a channel for divine blessings—a murti,"[62] says religion lecturer Paul Gwynne. In the presence

Hindu worshippers gather at a temple. Hindus are tolerant and accepting of various religious views, making India one of the world's most religiously diverse and spiritually active countries.

of a murti, Hindus consider themselves in the presence of the actual god or goddess. They believe every murti, regardless of the deity it shows, holds the presence of God.

Although not every image of a Hindu deity is a murti, murtis are widespread throughout the Hindu world. Some are giant statues. Others show gods or goddesses as the size of human beings. There are also small murtis that are portable, because Hindus like to keep murtis of their chosen gods within their homes or businesses so they can worship throughout the day. Whether a murti is a statue or a framed painting, however, it is a sacred object to a Hindu, no matter which deity it portrays. "In most Hindu traditions, the sacred image is an integral component of ritual adoration," Gwynne says. "It is the center of attention and the heart of all symbolic acts during the service."[63]

Temples: Homes for Murtis

Hindus see murtis as a physical presence of God, and just as there are precise rules for making a murti, there are rules for worshipping them. This is often done in a mandir, a Hindu temple that houses one or more murtis. All Hindu towns and cities are supposed to have at least one mandir. In towns and villages mandirs are often just small shrines representing a single deity—the local favorite. Cities, however, usually have mandirs for many different deities, and these temples can be very large and elaborate.

Whether small or large, most mandirs share certain features. On the outside there is usually an image of the deity for which the temple or shrine was built. A murti of Ganesha also appears near the entrance to many mandirs, because Hindus believe he removes obstacles to worship and makes a visitor's prayers easier for the deities to hear and answer. Mandirs are often elaborately decorated with paintings or carvings of deities and with architectural elements like spires and fancy gates.

Murtis of the featured deities are the centerpiece of any Hindu temple, and most mandirs employ a staff to look after them. "In every respect, the god or goddess is treated as a royal guest and given lavish hospitality and entertainment to foster intimacy between deity and devotee,"[64] says religion lecturer Mark W. Muesse. Since murtis are considered divine beings, they are dressed and decorated with jewels and flowers first thing in the morning in order to accept visitors during the day. Their clothes are changed again at night for rest. Murtis also receive food such as dried fruit during the day, just as any honored guest would be served meals. Tending to the needs of the murtis and the devotees who come to see them is a big job. Large temples may have hundreds of staff members.

Temples are sacred and popular for Hindus, but they have fewer rules than do the places of worship for many other religions. Many temples have particular prayer times or worship services, but others have no such formal gatherings. Most Hindus visit temples whenever they wish to feel closer to their favorite deity or if they have a favor to ask of a particular goddess or god. Visitors are mostly free to come and go as they choose during the day and to stay as long as they like. "There is no formal obligation for Hindus to visit the temple," says Indian and Hinduism historian Klaus K. Klostermaier, "but there would hardly be any Hindu who would not go to the temple once in a while."[65]

Hindus also have home shrines—sometimes an entire room but often just a shelf or altar—where they set up small murtis of their chosen deities. Just as in a mandir, families share meals with their murtis and worship them at home, often several times a day. For most Hindus, worshipping at home is as important as temple worship. "Because Hinduism is family oriented and home based, shrines in the home have a significant role," say religion and humanities professors Gurinder Singh Mann, Paul Numrich, and Raymond Williams. "Indeed, the home shrine is an authentic residence of the gods and the site of most Hindu rituals, so it is possible to be an observant Hindu and rarely visit a temple."[66] Between temples and home shrines, there are a wide variety of murtis and worship practices throughout the Hindu world.

Hindu Celebrations

Whether acts of devotion take place at home or in temples, there is often a spirit of celebration and joy in the worship of Hindu gods. Different denominations have different holy days, and not all Hindus take part in every festival, but in India, religious celebrations are frequent occasions. "It is believed that Indians have more festivals than any other culture,"[67] says education professor Brad Olsen.

Hindus typically have great love and admiration for their favorite deities and celebrate them with a joy and exuberance that is contagious even to non-Hindus. Says Klostermaier:

> The basic structure of the festival is quite simple: usually it is a procession in which the *murti* is taken through town. But what makes it such an interesting experience is *how* this is done. . . . Many thousands of people gather days ahead; they camp out on the roadside, squat together in picturesque groups . . . roam the streets, loudly singing their religious songs—and wait for the great occasion.[68]

Hindu festivals may last for one day or for several. Observers take time off from their jobs or other day-to-day responsibilities to feast, visit with relatives and friends, attend plays and other performances, dance, buy new clothes, and decorate their houses, streets, and temples. The most popular festivals are related to the major denominations of Hinduism. The births of Rama and Krishna, the two most popular avatars of

Visiting a Hindu Temple

People visit Hindu temples primarily to see murtis, statues they believe are infused with the spirit of God. Satguru Bodhinatha Veylanswami, head of the Hindu monastery in Kauai, Hawaii, explains murtis this way: "If we want to see a distant galaxy, we can go to an observatory and look through a powerful telescope. To see into the nucleus of a cell, we go to a laboratory and use a microscope. Similarly, to know God, we can go to the temple and experience Divinity through the sanctified murti."

Most temples welcome visitors, even if they are not Hindu, but certain behavior is expected of everyone:

- Temple visitors should bathe or shower before their visit and wear clean, nice, and modest clothing.
- Visitors should ring a bell when they arrive to announce their presence to temple staff and the deities within.
- Shoes are never worn inside a temple. Most temples have racks or shelves outside to hold shoes.
- Visitors usually rinse their hands and face in bathing pools or fountains before entering the temple.

- It is customary to bring an offering, such as flowers for the deity or money for the temple collection box.
- Most temples have a statue of Ganesha near the entrance, and visitors visit or pray to him before going in.
- Inside the temple visitors may circumambulate, or walk clockwise, around the central altar that holds the murti.
- Men and women usually sit apart during a temple service.
- If sitting on the floor, visitors should not point their feet at a deity or at another person, since this is a sign of disrespect.
- Following a service, *prasada* is handed out to worshippers. This is a small piece of food that was offered to and blessed by the deity. By accepting the *prasada*, a visitor accepts the deity's blessing.

Satguru Bodhinatha Veylanswami. "Educational Insight: Visiting a Hindu Temple." *Hinduism Today Magazine*, October /November/December 2012. www.hinduismtoday.com /modules/smartsection/item.php?itemid=5315.

A Hindu ceremony takes place inside a temple in India.

the god Vishnu, are occasions for major celebrations. So are major victories or accomplishments from the myths of the warrior goddesses Durga and Kali. Other festivals are seasonal or honor famous gurus, human spiritual guides Hindus believe to have been especially important.

Some Hindu festivals are so popular that they are observed worldwide and are known even to people who are not Hindu. One such celebration is Holi, a springtime festival in honor of Vishnu that takes place each March during a full moon. People decorate with flowers and bright colors. As they sing, dance, and feast in the streets during Holi, Hindus take great delight in spraying each other with dyed water in bright colors that symbolize the joy and fertility of spring.

Diwali, the festival of lights, is another Hindu celebration widely known around the world. Diwali commemorates the return of Rama and his wife, Sita, heroes of *The Ramayana*, after fourteen years of exile. Observed during the fall harvest, this festival also honors Lakshmi, the goddess of wealth and prosperity. Diwali features bonfires and fireworks, and people decorate homes, streets, and public buildings with lanterns and strings of light. "Diwali is a night to see with all the homes and buildings glittering with lights," says business professor Francisca O. Norales. "All Indian people, irrespective of rank and status, are imbued with a festive spirit."[69] Feasts, family visits, and gift exchanges are major features of Diwali, which is as special and important to Hindus as Christmas is to Christians and Hanukkah is to Jews.

A Personalized Faith

Hindus bring joy and excitement to their worship practices through festivals that unite people in peace and friendship and through their loving worship of murtis, whom they treat as family members and friends. They seek a personal relationship with the divine being, and their myths, epic stories, and daily religious practices all share the goal of knowing and understanding God. Hinduism's status as the oldest of the world's surviving faiths may be the result of its personable approach to religion, something that helps it continuously appeal to its followers and keeps it relevant to people living in the modern world.

CHAPTER 5

Modern Hinduism Around the World

Hinduism is the third-largest religion in the world today. With nearly 1 billion followers, it is behind only Christianity (with 2.1 billion followers worldwide) and Islam (with 1.6 billion followers) and is growing at a rate of 1.52 percent per year. The rapid rise in the number of Hindus is mostly because the population of India itself is growing faster than any other nation in the world, and 80 percent of India's people are Hindu. About 98 percent of all the world's Hindus live on the Indian subcontinent. However, millions of people from India have also migrated to Western nations and taken Hindu beliefs and customs with them. In North America, for example, 1.5 percent of Canadians identify themselves as Hindu, and in the United States 0.4 percent of the population—about 1.2 million people—say they are Hindus.

The United States is home to thousands of Hindu temples that serve the growing American Hindu population, which is especially concentrated in California and in northeastern states like New York and New Jersey—although there is at least one Hindu center in every state. "My own sense of the future is we are going to see a certain flourishing of the Hindu tradition in the United States,"[70] says Anant Rambachan, chair of the Religion Department at St. Olaf College in Northfield, Minnesota.

The religious beliefs, ideas, and customs of Hindus are vastly different than those of Christians, who make up 77 percent of the American population, but the United States is a nation of religious freedom where Hindus are welcome to practice their beliefs. Hinduism, likewise, is an open-minded religion that generally exists peacefully alongside other faiths. Hindus do not see it as their duty to convert people of other faiths to Hinduism, but they are welcoming of outsiders who are interested in their beliefs. Throughout history, people have been inspired by the ideas of Hinduism, and the trend continues today. Many Hindu concepts, beliefs, and practices have gained a significant following in the popular culture of the West, especially in the United States.

The Idea of Past and Future Lives

One of the most popular Hindu ideas is reincarnation, a concept that is discussed in the Vedas and is thought to be several thousand years old. Hindus (along with believers of many other religions, including modern-day Buddhists, and the ancient Greeks) believe that when a person's physical body dies, the soul moves to a different physical form and begins a new life. In other words, it reincarnates, or inhabits a new body of flesh. Thus, to Hindus, death is not permanent but a new beginning, a necessary part of the cycle of dying and being reborn. This helps explain why Hindus believe that their epic human heroes, Rama and Krishna, are one and the same being. It also explains why Hindus revere the destroyer god Shiva and the death goddess Kali, because without death, the soul cannot be reborn to its next form.

Many people outside of Hinduism are also attracted to the idea of reincarnation. For one thing, it lessens the fear of dying and of losing loved ones. Hindus tend to accept such situations quietly because they know that death is inevitable but also because they believe it is not permanent. The soul will have more chances in future lives to finish whatever was not completed in this one.

Goddess of Rock

The logo of the Rolling Stones, a popular American rock band that formed in the 1960s and is still active today, is a red mouth with a protruding tongue set against a black background. The design was inspired by the mouth of the powerful and unconventional Hindu goddess Kali.

Most Americans' religious beliefs do not involve reincarnation, but nevertheless, they often speak of things that must have happened in a past life or what they hope to accomplish in a future one. In the early 1900s, automobile pioneer Henry Ford was an early American believer in the idea. "When I discovered Reincarnation it was as if I had found a universal plan," he said. "I realised that there was a chance to work out my ideas. Time was no longer limited. I was no longer a slave to the hands of the clock."[71] Many Americans find the Hindu idea of reincarnation as attractive as Ford did. According to a December 2013 Harris poll, about one in four Americans claims to believe in past and future lives.

This Hindu temple is in Malibu, California. Approximately 1.2 million practicing Hindus reside in the United States.

Getting One's Just Deserts

To Hindus the concept of reincarnation goes hand in hand with the idea that thoughts and actions have consequences. Hindus believe in karma, a cause-and-effect cycle in which

Born Again

Many Hindu myths involve reincarnation, or the rebirth of a soul into different physical bodies. In 1930 in Delhi, India, a girl named Shanti Devi seemed to provide evidence of this phenomenon. At age four Devi began to talk of her past life as a woman named Lugdi who had lived in a town many miles away and had died during childbirth. Devi's parents were skeptical for years, but the girl's insistence eventually prompted her schoolteachers to look up Kedarnath, the man Devi said was her former husband. Not only did Kedarnath exist, he lived in the town Devi had named, and his wife, Lugdi, had died during childbirth the year before Devi was born. Kedarnath was told of the strange occurrence. He went to visit Devi but posed as his own brother. Devi not only knew the difference, she began to talk with Kedarnath about private details of their life together that only Lugdi would have known.

Many people interviewed Devi during her life, but not once was she known to change her story or give a false detail about Lugdi. She died unmarried in 1987 at age sixty-one. Her story remains famous today as a possible example of a true reincarnation.

the things a person says, thinks, and does build up into a force that will affect the experiences he or she has in this life and in lives to come. Kind and honest thoughts and deeds bring about positive experiences, whereas selfish or cruel thinking and behavior lead to negative outcomes. Hindus believe that karma, both good and bad, accumulates during each lifetime and moves with the soul into all future lives. Any negative karma created now is certain to bring unpleasantness later on. A person with an especially large amount of bad karma, for example, may be reborn as a person with a low status in society or even as an animal.

One Hindu myth relates a conversation between the sage Vyasa and an insect in the road. "I was a sudra [a member of the working class] in my former birth," the insect says.

"But since I did not respect the brāhmans [holy men] and guests and possessed many bad qualities like anger, cruelty, cunningness, greed, jealousy, etc., I was born as an insect."[72] Vyasa tells the insect how to live righteously so that he can improve his status in future lives. "The insect followed the advice of the sage and was born successively as a porcupine, a pig, a deer, a bird, and then a human being,"[73] the myth says. Eventually, he lived so honorably that he achieved what Hindus believe is the ultimate goal of existence—freedom from the cycle of rebirth.

Hindus believe good thoughts and deeds can soften the effects of bad ones. Karma is like a bank account into which the soul makes positive and negative deposits. Over time, by trying to live virtuously in each life, a soul's good karma will outweigh the bad, so future lives will improve and the person will have better fortune. Hindus believe that unhappy circumstances such as illness happen to people because of bad karma they accumulated in previous lives, whereas people who seem blessed with good fortune are reaping the benefits of good behavior in past lives. Everyone, however, can

The tale of the Hindu god Vyasa (shown) and the the insect reveals the Hindu concept of reincarnation, which relates to karma, the belief that all actions have consequences.

constantly improve their circumstances with good thoughts and behavior, no matter what their situation in their current life. Karma is a forgiving concept, since even seemingly bad people can redeem themselves by behaving better.

The phrases "good karma" and "bad karma" are widely used and understood in the United States. Even people who do not believe in reincarnation may find themselves adjusting their behavior, perhaps even superstitiously, so they will build up good karma in life rather than bad. "Many Americans and Europeans actually adopt reincarnation and karma concepts, not to replace, but to augment, their more traditional Christian and Jewish beliefs,"[74] says spiritualism scholar Norman C. McClelland.

Exercising the Hindu Way

Just as concepts like karma and reincarnation are becoming more familiar to people in the West, so is a Hindu custom called yoga, a physical exercise that combines specific body postures with controlled breathing and concentration to help people unify their body, mind, and spirit. Calming and silencing the mind in order to focus on inner peace is part of meditation and has been a Hindu practice for thousands of years. Artifacts found in India that date back five millennia show artwork of people in yoga poses still practiced today. Hinduism is not the only religion to practice yoga (it is a common activity among Buddhists, too, for example), and not all Hindus take part in yoga. However, yoga is strongly linked to the Hindu concept of achieving *moksha*, or liberation—separating the spiritual self from the physical self, which is the ultimate goal of all Hindus and the only way to free oneself from the cycle of reincarnation.

Yoga has always had an important role in Hindu mythology. Hindus consider Shiva the first yogi, or yoga instructor, and also the patron god of yoga. Many images of Shiva show him with his eyes closed and his legs crossed, the yoga pose known as seated meditation. The goal of one type of yoga, called Shiva yoga, is to help people open their spiritual third eye—the eye that, like Shiva's, can look inward to the soul. In Hindu mythology the practice of yoga is tied to spiritual worship, especially the worship of Shiva. "The supreme

being in the form of Shiva is credited with the authorship of yoga," says yoga instructor Gregor Maehle. "Many myths about the origin of yoga start with a dialogue between him and the mother of the universe . . . Parvati."[75]

Many yoga positions, or asanas, are named for Hindu deities. Krishnasana and Ramasana, for example, are named after Krishna and Rama, the most popular avatars of the god Vishnu. Another pose, Hanumanasana, is named after the monkey-god Hanuman. Popular chants repeated during some yoga classes also mention Hindu gods, such as "*Om Namah Shivaaya,*" which translates to "I bow to the Lord Shiva."[76] For Hindus, yoga is a distinctly spiritual practice.

However, during the recent spread of yoga to the Western world, its ties to Hinduism have not always been recognized. A 2012 study by the Harris Interactive Service Bureau showed that about 20 million people in the United States—more than 8 percent of Americans—practiced yoga, an increase of 29 percent since 2008. Yoga is especially popular among American women, who make up 82 percent of practitioners. Yoga has become a major industry in the

These Hindus practice yoga, a way to unify the body, mind, and spirit and unite oneself with God. Many systems of yoga exist and can include specific body postures with controlled breathing and concentrated attention, as well as meditation.

United States, where people spend $27 billion per year on yoga-related classes, retreats, clothing, and accessories. Most Americans, though, practice yoga to get stronger or leaner, not as a spiritual exercise. Yoga is one of the most visible ways Hindu beliefs and practices have affected the Western world and also one of the most controversial.

Some American practitioners of yoga deny that it is a form of Hindu worship at all. "Yoga is not a religion," says the American Yoga Association. "It has no creed or fixed set of beliefs, nor is there a prescribed godlike figure to be worshipped in a particular manner . . . the common belief that Yoga derives from Hinduism is a misconception."[77] Hindus, on the other hand, claim that yoga is strongly tied to Hinduism and that spirituality *is* the most important goal of yoga. "Ignored are both the moral basis of the practice and the ultimate spiritual goal," the Hindu American Foundation says. "Second, there is the concerning trend of disassociating yoga from its Hindu roots. Both yoga magazines and studios assiduously present Yoga as an ancient practice independent and disembodied from the Hinduism that gave forth this immense contribution to humanity."[78] The debate about whether yoga is primarily spiritual or just a good workout is likely to continue as more and more Westerners take up this meditative form of exercise.

Hinduism, Science, and the Origins of Humanity

The spread of Hindu ideas and practices like karma and yogic meditation is not a new phenomenon. Hindu practices and ways of thinking have influenced other cultures for thousands of years. Hindus, in fact, claim that their culture was the origin of all others. Myths and stories in the Vedas, the original Hindu texts, tell of the creation of the gods, the world, and the first human beings, who dwelled in modern-day India and gave rise to all the other cultures that have existed through time.

Hinduism is not the only religion to claim that its people were the first. The Bible, for example, says that the first man and woman were Adam and Eve and came from the Garden of Eden, which biblical scholars believe was located between the Tigris and Euphrates Rivers in the Middle East. For hundreds of years, scientists and religion scholars have believed that creation stories like these are impossible to prove. The Hindu myths, especially, were believed to be historically inaccurate because many of them mention certain rivers and cities of which no trace existed.

As science has become more advanced, however, some significant discoveries in India have shown there may be some truth to certain Hindu myths. In the early to mid-1800s, railroad workers in northern India came across traces of crumbled brick ruins near the Indus River. In the 1920s archaeologists went to India to excavate the sites. They unearthed the remains of two ancient cities, Harappa and Mohenjo-Daro.

These settlements, arranged in grid systems, were large for their time. They had toilet facilities and contained granaries to hold stores of grain for their citizens. Such carefully planned cities were far more advanced than archaeologists had expected. These were not primitive villages. They had been purposefully built by a civilization that must already have been quite advanced, meaning the culture that created them was likely far older than the cities themselves. "These findings astounded Western archaeologists, but orthodox Hindus weren't surprised at all," says Hinduism author and lecturer Linda Johnsen. "Their ancient chronicles—enormous religious anthologies like the Puranas and the *Mahabharata* . . . often mentioned glorious cities of the ancient past."[79]

After analyzing the molecules of artifacts like pottery and bricks dug up at Harappa and Mohenjo-Daro, archaeologists determined these ancient cities in India were probably built around 7500 B.C., making India the home of some of the most ancient human artifacts ever discovered. These findings agree with other scientific evidence that supports the Vedic claims that Hinduism has been around for many millennia. The Vedas, for example, describe star patterns and arrangements that modern astronomers know would have appeared in the night sky during a period many thousands of years ago but not since.

The discovery of the five-thousand-year-old city of Harappa in the 1920s revealed a sophisticated culture and supported the claim that Hinduism has been around for millennia.

Many Vedic stories also tell of a mighty river called the Saraswati, with ties to the goddess of creativity and learning who goes by the same name. No such river currently exists where the Vedas indicate it should be. However, modern satellite photos clearly show the remains of a massive river in the Indian subcontinent, a river scientists now believe dried up about 4000 B.C. "So there it was," says Johnsen, "the [Saraswati] river the Veda had been talking about—just exactly where the Veda had always said it was."[80]

Scientific discoveries have shown that Hindu myths long believed to be folklore could be based on things that really existed or happened in ancient times. This is another way Hinduism has affected the modern world—scientists and historians regularly visit the subcontinent and read ancient Hindu texts for clues about the history not just of Hindu culture but of mankind. As new discoveries give credibility to some of the favorite stories Hindus have always shared and believed in, these stories gain popularity and are retold in modern media for modern Hindu audiences.

Hinduism in the Movies

Scientific discoveries during the past two centuries give credence to many stories Hindus have passed down from generation to generation, but the spread of their most beloved myths to modern generations has had more to do with technology than archaeology. Epic adventures like those of *The Mahabharata* and *The Ramayana* are a natural fit for movie screens, something India has in abundance. India has a filmmaking tradition nearly as old as that of the United States, and it produces hundreds of films and movies every year in the many different native languages of India. The city of Mumbai on the west coast of India (called Bombay until 1995) is home to the world-renowned Hindu film industry, known as Bollywood because it is Bombay's equivalent to America's Hollywood. Among the people of India, it has been just as successful.

The first feature-length Bollywood film, made in 1913, was *Raja Harishchandra*. This cinematic version of the story of Harishchandra, a hero of the Hindu epic *The Mahabharata*, was a silent film, like its Hollywood counterparts of the era. By the 1930s Hindu films had sound, and India had movie stars. Millions of people turned out to watch tales of their favorite epic heroes and original stories, too, all acted out on lavish, colorful backdrops with dashing costumes and singing actors and actresses.

Bollywood movies are one of India's most popular pastimes and have as

Devoted to Cinema

In 2009 Bollywood—India's movie industry—sold 3.2 billion tickets, far outdoing Hollywood's 1.4 billion ticket sales for the same year.

Bollywood films have helped give Indians a sense of unity and cultural pride and often feature stories of epic Hindu heroes who had to struggle to find their rightful place in the world.

much cultural importance there as movies have in the United States. In the 1940s, when India was struggling for independence from England, Bollywood films helped give the native people a sense of unity and cultural pride and often featured stories of epic Hindu heroes who themselves had struggled to find their rightful place in the world. Bollywood movies tend to be both musical and melodramatic, and they are often hits at international film festivals. Recently, global film companies like 20th Century Fox, Warner Brothers, and Sony Pictures have started investing in India's massive and profitable film industry.

Today, in an era of special effects and digital sound, Bollywood films come in all genres, including action, romance,

thrillers, and comedy, but the influence of Hinduism is often easy to find. "For the most part, the traditions and rituals promoted so heavily in Bollywood films tend to be derived from Hindu mythology and symbolism,"[81] says communications professor Faiza Hirji. Many Bollywood movies, in fact, are direct retellings of favorite episodes in Hindu folklore. One example is the 2010 movie *Raavan*, a retelling of the Hindu epic *The Ramayana*, in which the main character's love interest is kidnapped and held hostage by a demonic villain. Another recent Bollywood film with ties to Hindu folklore is 2013's science-fiction superhero film *Krrish*, which tells of a young man who develops the godlike powers of Krishna. However, even when Bollywood storylines seem to have no direct ties to Hinduism, scripts and movie soundtracks often mention Hindu gods or goddesses or feature characters praying to deities or to murtis.

Much of Hinduism's influence on Bollywood also happens offscreen, in the form of directors and actors working with personal gurus (religious experts) during the making of a movie and praying to their favorite gods for good fortune in the days before a film's release. Bollywood directors also choose the release dates for their films based on the *muhurat* of their favorite deity—a time period when planetary objects are believed to line up in a way that makes a deity particularly powerful. For followers of that deity, major activities (like a movie release) that are begun during the *muhurat* are thought to have the best possible chance for success. Bollywood directors' careful choice of movie release dates is one more way spiritual beliefs have an influence in the modern Hindu world.

Hinduism in Hollywood

Hollywood films are not as popular in India as in the United States, and similarly, Bollywood movies tend to lack the popularity in the United States that they have in India. American movies with Hindu themes and settings are therefore rare, but one famous example, Steven Spielberg's 1984 blockbuster *Indiana Jones and the Temple of Doom*, spread many stereotypes about Hindu beliefs and customs. In the movie archaeologist Indiana Jones's plane crashes in an Indian jungle, and local villagers beg him to bring back the sacred stone that has been stolen from their village. The stone is actually a Shiva Linga, a sacred symbol to Shaiva Hindus. Jones's quest takes him to the secret underground temple of a demonic, blood-drinking, human-sacrificing priest who chants to Kali, the Hindu goddess of death. After nearly losing his life and his soul, Jones defeats the evil priest and returns the stolen Shiva Linga to restore prosperity to the village.

This movie was criticized by Hindus for depicting Hindu culture as primitive and for suggesting that certain Hindus, particularly those who worship Shiva and the goddess Kali, have frightening and violent customs. "*Temple of Doom* engages in . . . blatant stereotyping,"[82] say sociology and English professors Hernán Vera and Andrew M. Gordon. In an attempt to portray Indian culture, they say, the movie actually insults it by implying that "twentieth-century Indians eat monkey brains; indulge in devil worship, unspeakable rituals, and human sacrifice; and exploit children as slave labor."[83] However incorrect its portrayal of the Hindu culture may have been, *The Temple of Doom* was a major hit for American movie audiences and therefore may have spread many false ideas.

Spielberg, the American-born director of *The Temple of Doom*, is not a Hindu, but in the 1990s American film audiences welcomed a new director who is Hindu. M. Night Shyamalan was born in India but moved with his family to Philadelphia, Pennsylvania, when he was a boy. After studying film at New York University, Shyamalan made his first major film in 1999, a supernatural thriller called *The Sixth Sense*. Other Shyamalan blockbusters have included *Unbreakable* in 2000 and *Signs* in 2002, both sporting the supernatural elements and unexpected plot twists that have become signature features of Shyamalan's films—even if references to Hindu mythology have not.

However, certain Hindu themes do show up in Shyamalan's movies, such as second chances, discovering one's purpose in life, the inevitability of death, and belief in the possibility of supernatural things. Shyamalan's films have not featured Hindu gods or myths directly, but many people do find something mystical in them. "There is . . . a loosely defined spirituality to Shyamalan's movies," says journalist Anthony Sacramone, "faith that you have a purpose and that you will never be at peace until you find that purpose."[84] For many Hindus, this is also a theme of their religion.

Stories of the Past and Future

From ancient texts to the big screen, Hinduism has captivated the people of India for many thousands of years. As India's population grows and spreads, Hinduism—long a misunderstood religious practice that seems at odds with the world's other major faiths—is reaching more corners of the world than ever before. The tales Hindus tell to define themselves and their beliefs are often thought by outsiders to have little relevance to the modern world. However, Hindus'

On Strike for Rama

One of the most significant events in television history happened in India from January 1987 to July 1988. Every Sunday morning during this time period, a television series aired that told the story of *The Ramayana*. One hundred million Hindus tuned in to watch, including many residents of rural villages who did not own a television and had to gather in homes of people who did. The series was so popular that it led to widespread public outrage in Jalandhar, a city in the state of Punjab, when the government—which originally had signed a contract for a year's worth of episodes—decided not to pay for the airing of the series finale. Government employees, especially sanitation workers, went on strike in protest. With no one collecting garbage, conditions grew so unsanitary that the government gave in and paid the producers of the TV series so it could air the end of the tale. The incident demonstrated the powerful connection between Hindus and their beloved epics.

most revered stories, both layered and symbolic, have not only survived countless encounters with other cultures, they have left a colorful impression.

Hindu mythology is full of heroes and villains, epic battles, betrayal, and true love. The gods and goddesses who populate these stories are just as popular today as they were in ancient times. As the rest of the world becomes more familiar with the deeply mystical Hindu faith, its myths intrigue whole new audiences of people with their exciting tales of heroism and moral choices. The stories are among mankind's oldest, but they still have great significance to almost one billion Hindus today.

Introduction: The Mythical World of Hinduism

1. Leviticus 26:1. New King James Version.

Chapter One: Life on the Indian Subcontinent

2. Georg Feuerstein, Subhash Kak, and David Frawley. *In Search of the Cradle of Civilization: New Light on Ancient India*. Wheaton, IL: Quest, 2001, p. 12.
3. Wendy Doniger. *The Hindus: An Alternative History*. New York: Oxford University, 2010, p. 62.
4. Bobbie Kalman. *India: The Land*. New York: Crabtree, 2010, p. 9.
5. Edwin Bernbaum and Larry W. Price. "Attitudes Toward Mountains." In *Mountain Geography: Physical and Human Dimensions*, edited by Martin Price, Alton Byers, Donald Friend, Thomas Kohler, and Larry W. Price. Berkeley: University of California, 2013, p. 261.
6. Shantha N. Nair. *The Holy Himalayas: An Abode of Hindu Gods*. New Delhi, India: Hindoology, 2007, p. 15.
7. Graham Phillips. *Alexander the Great: Murder in Babylon*. London: Virgin, 2004, p. 132.

8. Paul Vauthier Adams, Erick D. Langer, Lily Hwa, Peter N. Stearns, and Merry E. Wiesner-Hanks. *Experiencing World History*. New York: New York University, 2000, p. 132.
9. Adams et al. *Experiencing World History*, p. 134.
10. Linda Johnsen. *The Complete Idiot's Guide to Hinduism*. 2nd ed. New York: Alpha, 2009, p. 40.
11. Klaus K. Klostermaier. *A Survey of Hinduism*. 3rd ed. Albany: State University of New York, 2007, p. 400.
12. Penelope Carson. *The East India Company and Religion, 1698–1858*. Rochester, NY: Boydell, 2012, p. 4.
13. Jay Stevenson. *The Complete Idiot's Guide to Eastern Philosophy*. Indianapolis, IN: Alpha, 2000, pp. 102–103.
14. Des Cowley and Clare Williamson. *The World of the Book*. Melbourne, Australia: Miegunyah, 2007, p. 27.
15. Wendy Doniger. *The Hindus: An Alternative History*, p. 167.
16. Mahesh Sharma. *Tales from the Puranas*. New Delhi, India: Diamond Pocket, 2005, p. 7.
17. Kedar Nath Tiwari. *Classical Indian Ethical Thought: A Philosophical Study of Hindu, Jaina, and Bauddha Morals*. Delhi, India: Motilal Banarsidass, 2007, p. 54.

18. Louise Nicholson. *National Geographic Traveler: India*. 3rd ed. Washington, DC: National Geographic, 2010, p. 59.
19. Daniel J. Boorstin. *The Creators: A History of Heroes of the Imagination*. New York: Random House, 1993, p. 4.

Chapter Two: Hindu Gods and Goddesses

20. Bansi Pandit. *Explore Hinduism*. Loughborough, UK: Explore, 2005, p. 1.
21. Pandit. *Explore Hinduism*, p. 1.
22. James B. Robinson. *Hinduism*. New York: Chelsea House, 2004, p. 43.
23. Kailash Nath Seth and B.K. Chaturvedi. *Gods and Goddesses of India*. New Delhi, India: Diamond Pocket, 2000, p. 25.
24. Seth and Chaturvedi. *Gods and Goddesses of India*, p. 25.
25. T. Richard Blurton. *Hindu Art*. Cambridge, MA: Harvard University, 1993, p. 112.
26. Diana L. Eck. *Banaras, City of Light*. New York: Columbia University, 1993, p. 97.
27. Eck. *Banaras, City of Light*, p. 103.
28. Lynn Foulston and Stuart Abbott. *Hindu Goddesses: Beliefs and Practices*. Portland, OR: Sussex Academic, 2009, pp. 2–3.
29. Priya Hemenway. *Hindu Gods: The Spirit of the Divine*. San Francisco: Chronicle, 2003, p. 24.
30. Hemenway. *Hindu Gods*, p. 24.
31. Sally Kempton. *Awakening Shakti: The Transformative Power of the Goddesses of Yoga*. Boulder, CO: Sounds True, 2013, p. 179.
32. Karen Tate. *Sacred Places of Goddess: 108 Destinations*. San Francisco: Consortium of Collective Consciousness, 2006, p. 196.
33. Kempton. *Awakening Shakti*, pp. 106–107.
34. David R. Kinsley. *Hindu Goddesses: Visions of the Divine Feminine in the Hindu Religious Tradition*. Berkeley: University of California, 1988, p. 47.
35. Foulston and Abbott. *Hindu Goddesses*, p. 34.
36. Foulston and Abbott. *Hindu Goddesses*, p. 31.

Chapter Three: Hindu Heroes and Epic Tales

37. Madasamy Thirumalai. *Sharing Your Faith with a Hindu*. Bloomington, MN: Bethany House, 2012. Google e-book, p. 3.
38. Bulbul Sharma. *The Ramayana*. New Delhi, India: Puffin, 2003, p. 20.
39. Sharma. *The Ramayana*, p. 118.
40. Philip Wilkinson and Neil Philip. *Eyewitness Companions: Mythology*. New York: DK, 2007, p. 165.
41. Pankaj Mishra. "Introduction." In *The Ramayana: A Shortened Modern Prose Version of the Indian Epic*, edited by R.K. Narayan. New York: Penguin, 2006, p. viii.
42. Lakshmi Bandlamudi. *Dialogics of Self, the Mahabharata and Culture: The History of Understanding and Understanding of History*. New York: Anthem, 2011, p. 3.
43. Quoted in Barbara Miller. *The Bhagavad-Gita: Krishna's Counsel in Times of War*. New York: Bantam Dell, 2004, p. 7.

44. Quoted in Miller. *The Bhagavad-Gita*, p. 11.
45. Bandlamudi. *Dialogics of Self, the Mahabharata and Culture*, p. 189.
46. Ithamar Theodor. *Exploring the Bhagavad Gitā: Philosophy, Structure, and Meaning*. Burlington, VT: Ashgate, 2010, p. 1.
47. Philip Lutgendorf. *Hanuman's Tale: The Messages of a Divine Monkey*. New York: Oxford University, 2007, p. xii.
48. Lutgendorf. *Hanuman's Tale*, p. xiv.
49. Paul B. Courtright. "On This Day in My Humble Way: Aspects of Puja." In *Gods of Flesh, Gods of Stone: The Embodiment of Divinity in India*, edited by Joanne Punzo Waghorne, Norman Cutler, and Vasudha Narayanan. New York: Columbia University, 1996, pp. 34–35.
50. Courtright. "On This Day in My Humble Way," p. 34.
51. Johnsen. *Complete Idiot's Guide to Hinduism*, p. 182.
52. Feuerstein, Kak, and Frawley. *In Search of the Cradle of Civilization*, p. 229.

Chapter Four: Worshipping the Pantheon of Hindu Gods

53. Ninian Smart. *The World's Religions*. 2nd ed. New York: Cambridge University, 1998, p. 44.
54. Amrutur V. Srinivasanp. *Hinduism for Dummies*. Hoboken, NJ: Wiley, 2011, p. 52.
55. Vensus A. George. *Paths to the Divine: Ancient and Indian*. Washington, DC: Council for Research in Values and Philosophy, 2008, p. 232.
56. Ajit Mookerjee. *Ritual Art of India*. Rochester, VT: Inner Traditions International, 1998, p. 93.
57. Ginette Ishimatsu. "Tamil Shaivism." In *Religions of the World: A Comprehensive Encyclopedia of Beliefs and Practices*, 2nd ed., edited by J. Gordon Melton and Martin Baumann. Santa Barbara, CA: ABC-CLIO, 2010, p. 2809.
58. Prem P. Bhalla. *Hindu Gods and Goddesses*. New Delhi, India: Pustak Mahal, 2007, p. 45.
59. Carlos Lopez. "Shaktism." In *Religions of the World: A Comprehensive Encyclopedia of Beliefs and Practices*, 2nd ed., edited by J. Gordon Melton and Martin Baumann. Santa Barbara, CA: ABC-CLIO, 2010, p. 2600.
60. Stefano Mercanti. *The Rose and the Lotus: Partnership Studies in the Works of Raja Rao*. New York: Rodopi, 2009, p. 8.
61. Editors of *Hinduism Today Magazine*. *What Is Hinduism? Modern Adventures into a Profound Global Faith*. Kapaa, HI: Himalayan Academy, 2007, p. 313.
62. Paul Gwynne. *World Religions in Practice: A Comparative Introduction*. Malden, MA: Blackwell, 2011, p. 42.
63. Gwynne. *World Religions in Practice*, p. 42.
64. Mark W. Muesse. *The Hindu Traditions: A Concise Introduction*. Minneapolis, MN: Fortress, 2011, p. 141.
65. Klostermaier. *A Survey of Hinduism*, p. 277.
66. Gurinder Singh Mann, Paul Numrich, and Raymond Williams. *Buddhists, Hindus and Sikhs in America:*

A Short History. Oxford: Oxford University, 2008, pp. 62–63.

67. Brad Olsen. *Sacred Places Around the World: 108 Destinations.* 2nd ed. San Francisco: Consortium of Collective Consciousness, 2004, p. 90.

68. Klostermaier. *A Survey of Hinduism,* p. 277.

69. Francisca O. Norales. *Cross-Cultural Communication: Concepts, Cases and Challenges.* Youngstown, NY: Cambria, 2006. Kindle edition.

Chapter Five: Modern Hinduism Around the World

70. Quoted in David Briggs. "Hindu Americans: The Surprising, Hidden Population Trends of Hinduism in the U.S." *Huffington Post,* April 28, 2011. www.huffington post.com/david-briggs/first-hindu -census-reveal_b_853758.html.

71. Quoted in in Natasha Dern. "Do You Believe in Past Lives?" *Huffington Post,* May 10, 2010. www.huff ingtonpost.com/natasha-dern/do -you-believe-in-past-li_b_566665 .html.

72. Mariasusai Dhavamony. *Hindu Spirituality.* Rome: Gregorian Biblical BookShop, 1999, p. 175.

73. Dhavamony. *Hindu Spirituality,* p. 175.

74. Norman C. McClelland. *Encyclopedia of Reincarnation and Karma.* Jefferson, NC: McFarland, 2010, p. 6.

75. Gregor Maehle. *Ashtanga Yoga— the Intermediate Series: Mythology, Anatomy, and Practice.* Novato, CA: New World Library, 2009, p. 41.

76. *Yoga Journal.* "The Beginner's Guide to Common Chants." May 8, 2014. www.yogajournal.com/lifestyle/841.

77. American Yoga Association. "General Yoga Information," May 8, 2014. www.americanyogaassocia tion.org/general.html.

78. Hindu American Foundation. "Yoga Beyond Asana: Hindu Thought in Practice," May 8, 2014. http://hafsite.org/media/pr/yoga -hindu-origins.

79. Johnsen. *Complete Idiot's Guide to Hinduism,* p. 20.

80. Johnsen. *Complete Idiot's Guide to Hinduism,* p. 27.

81. Faiza Hirji. *Dreaming in Canadian: South Asian Youth, Bollywood, and Belonging.* Vancouver, BC: UBC, 2010, p. 116.

82. Hernán Vera and Andrew M. Gordon. *Screen Saviors: Hollywood Fictions of Whiteness.* Lanham, MD: Rowman & Littlefield, 2003, p. 36.

83. Vera and Gordon. *Screen Saviors,* p. 38.

84. Anthony Sacramone. "Movies by M. Night Shyamalan." *First Things,* July 26, 2006. www.firstthings.com /web-exclusives/2006/07/movies -by-m-night-shyamalan.

GLOSSARY

Aranyaka: The section of each Veda meant to be studied during meditation.

asana: A specific posture of yoga.

ascetic: Someone who practices severe self-discipline for religious reasons.

avatar: The form of a deity appearing in a physical body on earth, either as a person or an animal.

Brahman: The ultimate, divine Supreme Being that exists everywhere and within all things.

Brahmana: The section of each Veda that contains rituals or chants.

consort: The feminine counterpart of each of the Trimurti gods, personified as goddesses.

Devi: The female entity Shakti Hindus believed to be the Supreme Being.

dharma: A person's religious and moral duties that lead to personal contentment and universal balance.

guru: A spiritual teacher or master in Hinduism.

The Mahabharata: One of two epic Hindu poems; tells of a great battle between two families fighting over the same kingdom.

mandir: A Hindu temple or place of worship.

moksha: The release from the cycle of reincarnation as a result of building up good karma; for Hindus, the ultimate spiritual goal.

muhurat: A period when planetary objects line up in a way that makes a specific deity powerful.

murti: An image of a Hindu deity that is considered to hold the divine spirit.

pilgrimage: A religious journey, usually to a shrine or other sacred place, in search of moral or spiritual discovery.

Puranas: Sacred Hindu texts containing legends and folklore.

The Ramayana: One of two epic Hindu poems; tells the story of Rama's quest to rescue his wife from a demon.

reincarnation: The rebirth of the soul into a new physical body.

sage: A very wise guide or teacher.

Samhita: The section of each Veda that contains hymns.

Shaivism: The denomination of Hinduism that worships Shiva as the primary deity.

Shakti: The female source of energy in the universe.

Shaktism: The denomination of Hinduism that worships the Mother Goddess, also known as Shakti or Devi, as the primary deity.

shruti: The class of religious Hindu texts said to be based on direct revelation from the divine being.

Smartism: The denomination of Hinduism in which all gods are considered equal but that focuses especially on Shiva, Vishnu, Ganesha, Hanuman, Surya, and Murugan.

smriti: The class of religious Hindu texts said to be based on people's memory.

Trimurti: The three gods personifying the main functions of the universe: creation, preservation, and destruction.

Upanishad: The final section of each Veda, designed to help followers understand the relationship between themselves and the divine being.

Vaishnavism: The denomination of Hinduism that worships Vishnu as the primary deity.

Vedas: The most ancient sacred texts of Hinduism, arranged in four collections of verses that teach spiritual guidance and philosophy.

yoga: A spiritual Hindu practice that combines breathing, meditation, and specific bodily postures to relax and focus the mind.

Books

Sunita Pant Bansal. *Hindu Gods & Goddesses*. New Delhi, India: Smriti, 2005. Devotes a chapter each to major deities of Hinduism, plus one chapter to minor deities. Includes photographs and illustrations of deities, sacred sites, and artifacts.

Roshen Dalal. *Hinduism: An Alphabetical Guide*. London: Penguin UK, 2014. Gives brief descriptions of major and minor Hindu deities and defines terms and concepts described in Hinduism and its myths. Entries are arranged encyclopedia style, making this a good reference for reading about myths and deities.

R.K. Narayan. *The Mahabharata: A Shortened Modern Prose Version of the Indian Epic*. Chicago: University of Chicago Press, 2000. This retelling of the central story of *The Mahabharata*, written like a novel for English-speaking audiences instead of like an epic poem, includes all the major episodes and characters of the battle between two warring families of cousins.

R.K. Narayan. *The Ramayana: A Shortened Modern Prose Version of the Indian Epic*. New York: Penguin, 2006. Reading like a novel instead of an epic poem, this condensed and readable version of *The Ramayana* for an English-speaking audience includes all the major episodes and characters of the epic tale of Lord Rama in his quest to rescue his wife, Sita, from a demon.

Sue Penney. *Hinduism*. Chicago: Heinemann Library, 2008. Introduces major gods and goddesses and discusses common worship practices, sacred texts, and the history of the Hindu religion.

Internet Sources

HareKrishna. "Can You Name the Hindu Gods?" Sporcle. www.sporcle.com/games/HareKrishna/Hindu_Gods.

Angie McPherson. "Our Favorite Pictures from India's Holi Celebrations." *National Geographic*, March 18, 2014. http://news.nationalgeographic.com/news/2014/03/140318-holi-festival-colors-india-tradition-culture-2014.

Sivagami Natesan. "Diwali Deep in the Heart of Texas." *Hinduism Today Magazine*, April–June 2013. www.hinduismtoday.com/modules/smartsection/item.php?itemid=5369.

Websites

Encyclopedia Mythica (www.pantheon .org/areas/mythology). This website features major deities and mythological beliefs from all the continents. The Hinduism page provides a brief overview of the religion and an alphabetized list of dozens of Hindu deities, major and minor, each linked to articles, images, and explanations for visitors to explore.

Hindu Gods & Goddesses, Sanatan Society (www.sanatansociety.org /hindu_gods_and_goddesses.htm# .U3G8lleIOno). Features a gallery of deity images that, when clicked, take the visitor to further information about the god or goddess along with alternate forms, human avatars, significant myths, and more.

Hindu Gods & Goddesses, Useful Charts (www.usefulcharts.com/reli gion/main-hindu-gods-chart.html). Provides side-by-side images and basic facts about major Hindu dei-

ties to help draw connections in their relationships and make comparisons.

Hinduism, Religion Facts (www.reli gionfacts.com/hinduism). Gives an overview of many aspects of Hinduism, including culture and history, and also provides descriptions, illustrations, and explanations of symbolism for major Hindu deities.

Hindu Online (http://hinduonline.co /HinduReligion/HinduGods.html). Provides an overview of basic beliefs of Hinduism and features a large number of major and minor Hindu deities, with illustrations and descriptions of each.

***The Story of India*, PBS** (www.pbs.org /thestoryofindia). Designed to be used either in connection with the PBS television series *The Story of India* or alone, this website offers six lessons on Hinduism that students can do alone or in groups. Lessons include activities such as making a scrapbook of Hindu and Indian images or designing a Hindu monument.

INDEX

mother (Parvati), 40–41
of Shaktism, 64–66
of wealth/prosperity (Lakshmi),
37–39, 47, 48
Gurus, 52

H

Hanuman (monkey god), *51,*
51–53
Harappa (ancient city), 83, *84*
Harishchandra, 85
Harrison, George, 31
Himalayas, 13
Hindu American Foundation, 82
Hindu Civilization, map of, *4*
Hindu Trimurti, 28, *36*
Brahma, 28–31, *29*
goddesses and, 37
Shiva, 33–34, 36, *36*
Vishnu, 31–33, *32*
Hinduism, 8–9
beliefs/worldview of, 27–28,
43, 76
in Bollywood films, 85–87
family tree of major entities in,
5
four branches of, 60–61
in Hollywood films, 87–89
lotus and, 41
number of followers of, 75
pantheon of, *6,* 43
as personalized faith, 74
religious tolerance in, 67–68, 76
respect for scientific knowledge in,
58
sacred scriptures of, *22,* 23–24, 50,
66–67
Holi (springtime festival), 74

I

Iliad (Homer), 24
India
archaeological discoveries in, 83
under British colonization, 19–21
caste system in, 68
geography of, 11–13
Greek invasion of, 14–15
introduction of Islam into, 16–18
map of, *4*
Republic of, 21–22
Roman trade with, 15–16
Indiana Jones and the Temple of Doom
(film), 87–88
Indra (rain god), 57

K

Kali (dark goddess), 41–42, *42, 66,* 76
Karma, 68, 77–80
Kauravas (sons of demons), 48
Krishna (avatar of Vishnu), 48–49, *49,*
50, 57, 61, 76
Krrish (film), 87

L

Lakshmi (goddess of wealth/prosperity),
39–40, 61
Rama as human form of, 47, 48

M

The Mahabharata (epic poem), 24, 44,
47, 48–50
origin of, 54–55
Mandirs. *See* Temples

PICTURE CREDITS

Cover: © Paul Prescott/Shutterstock.com

© AFP/Getty Images, 56

© age fotostock Spain, S.L./Alamy, 73

© Allstar Picture Library/Alamy, 77

© The Art Archive/Wat Phra Keo, Royal Palace, Bangkok/Francoise Cazanave, 46

© Art Directors & TRIP/Alamy, 62, 79

© British Library/Robana via Getty images, 45

© Charles O. Cecil/Alamy, 25

© Dennis Campbell/Alamy, 29

© Dinodia Photos/Alamy, 21, 22, 30, 60

© FotoFlirt/Alamy, 55

© Gale/Cengage Learning, 4, 5, 6

© Hulton Archive/Getty Images, 19

© Image Broker/Alamy, 69

© Jane Sweeney/Robert Harding Picture Library Ltd./Alamy, 51

© Jerry Redfern/Getty Images, 66

© Kathy Willens/AP/Corbis, 8

© Louise Batalla Duran/Alamy, 38, 49, 65

© North Wind Picture Archives/Alamy, 15

© PhotoStock-Israel/Alamy, 12

© Robert Harding World Imagery/Alamy, 81, 84, 86

© Simon Reddy/Alamy, 42

© Universal Images Group Limited/Alamy, 35

© World Religions Photo Library/Alamy, 18, 32, 36, 70

ABOUT THE AUTHOR

Jenny MacKay is the author of more than twenty-five books for teens and preteens on topics such as crime scene investigation, sports science, social issues, and pop culture. She lives in Sparks, Nevada, with her husband, daughter, and son.